LEISURE
AND
PLEASURE
A MEDLEY OF SPARE TIME PURSUITS

By
The Women's Research Group

Published by The Women's Research Group
First Edition 2009

The Women's Research Group has been working to record the lives of women in Coventry since its foundation in 1998. It is important that the history of women in the city should not be forgotten. This book contains a light-hearted look at the way women used their leisure time in the twentieth century.

Previous books published by the Women's Research Group:

Redressing the Balance
Hurdy Gurdy Days
Keeping the Balance
Telling Tales
All in a Day's Work
Making the Best of Things

ISBN 978-0-9540604-5-9

CONTENTS

Acknowledgements

The Women's Research Group would like to thank the following organisations and individuals for their help in preparing this book.

The staff of Local Studies at Coventry Library and Information Services.

The staff of The History Centre, especially Andrew Mealey, for permission to reproduce photographs from The Loudspeaker and the picture of the Opera House.

Individuals who have supplied information and photographs of themselves, their relatives or buildings.

Girlguiding UK for permission to use the Guide badge on the front cover.

Disclaimer

We do everything possible to ensure that the information contained in these articles is correct. However, we are reliant upon the memories of the people we interview.

Every attempt has been made to ensure that the photographs produced in this book do not infringe copyright. The group has made every effort to locate all persons having any rights to photographs used.

Those Were The Days

Many of us, no doubt, were big filmgoers in the past; this was good entertainment and whiled away a few hours. Looking back there were many cinemas in Coventry as with other towns and cities, but sadly with the advent of television and videos, we choose to stay at home and usually nod off in the armchair. It was interesting to see that in 1911 parliament stopped shows being held in circus tents, due to fire hazard.

As a child I used to go to the *Plaza* in Spon End on a Saturday morning to 'Chums Club.' Before the film started there used to be a man on the stage called 'Uncle'. He led a sing-song. The films always seemed to be exciting, with the 'goodies and baddies', cowboys and Indians. There were science fiction and outer space films in the 1950s. The film always finished with a cliff-hanger, just to make sure that you went the following week to find out what happened. I think the charge was sixpence (2.5p). Should there happen to be a broken film the audience would boo and stamp their feet until it had been spliced. Usherettes would guide you to your seat carrying a torch, which did not give out much light, you really could not see where you were going and often ended up sitting on someone's lap (lucky girl)! During the interval they would stand at the front of the stage with a tray, hung around their neck selling ice cream, lit by a small bulb on the tray. Of course you always stood to attention at the end of the programme for the National Anthem. Some time later I can remember wearing cardboard spectacles with one red and one green lens to watch the Three Dimensional (3D) films. These films appeared to have wild animals, aeroplanes or ships jumping out at you, they were very realistic. However, the 3D fad did not last long as some viewers suffered eyestrain and headaches from watching them. If the projection was not done perfectly by the cinema, the film was just a blurred mess. As a result an ordinary film attracted more viewers than the 3D.

There were many cinemas in Coventry, but now there are just the *Skydome* (*Odeon*), and the *Showcase* at Walsgrave. These are what are termed multi-screen cinemas, in which there are various cinemas showing different films. It seems a different world now and you can purchase large bags of popcorn to munch throughout the film. The *Skydome* gives concessions to senior citizens one day a week and normally starts at mid-day. Included in the price of the ticket you can have a cup of tea or coffee and biscuits, which you take with you into the cinema and in the arm of your seat is a place in which you can put your cup. I know that this was not the case in the past. There is also a small cinema at Warwick University, which is very popular.

You may recall many of the cinemas listed below and no doubt you frequented them. In Earlsdon Street there was the *Imperial*, originally it was called the *Electric* this was opened on 5th December 1911, and because of its bareness inside it was nicknamed the barn. At that time, of course, it was only showing silent films. On 1st April 1930, the audience were able to see 'talkies' for the first time at this cinema. Before the films reached the *Imperial* they had been shown many times at other cinemas and were very well worn and a lot of breakdowns occurred. In the blitz of 1940 the cinema was bombed and was out of action for a time. As a child I went with my parents to see 'The Blue Lamp' featuring Jack Warner and Dirk Bogarde, this was the first film in England to show a policeman being shot; this film was launched in 1950. I also saw the 'The Song of Bernadette', which was released in 1943. Jennifer Jones the film's star was awarded the Golden Globe in 1944 for her acting ability; it also starred Vincent Price and Gladys Cooper.

In 1951 the *Imperial* became *La Continentale*, which showed only films from France, Italy, Spain and South American countries. The Lady Mayoress, Mrs Harry Weston did the honours by opening it. The cinema ran until 1960. It was then a private members film club with very strict rules and was not open to the public, it was called the *Moulin Rouge* and ran until 1962 and was demolished in 1965.

The *Broadway/Astoria* cinema was situated in Albany Road, Earlsdon, and was opened on 3rd November 1922 and was initially called the *Broadway*. At the grand opening the feature film was 'The Game of Life', apparently this was the longest running film until 1922. It was a silent film and an historical epic. Times of showing were twice nightly 6.30pm and 8.30pm and daily matinees at 3pm. Prices of admission were Grand Circle one shilling and sixpence (7.5p), Stalls one shilling (5p) and Pit Stalls nine pence (3.5p). The cinema boasted an elegant foyer, and furnished with a gas fire, oak panelled walls, big oak settles and potted palms. It was sold in

1929, to a London company who installed 'talkies' and then resold it in 1933 when its name changed to the *Astoria*. In 1944 one of the films shown was 'Wuthering Heights', starring Laurence Olivier and Merle Oberon. The chief projectionist was Bill Edkins and the second projectionist was Gladys Ward.

Astoria Cinema, now Nexus building.

Sadly, the cinema closed on 1st November 1959. The building is now used by Nexus, as a theatre and music recording Studio College.

Hillfields had four cinemas in the past; it just shows how popular picture houses were. Hillfields first cinema was the *Coronet* in Paynes Lane. It opened in 1910 on the site of the former Coronet works, but it closed three years later in 1913. Later it became a D.I.Y Warehouse, this closed in the early 1980s, to make way for Sky Blue Way. The *Palladium Picture Palace*, in King William Street, was opened in 1915 and was one of Mr. Pell's cinemas. It stayed open until 1962, when it was purchased by a company to show Asian films. There was a fire in 1971 and the cinema closed again until 1983. It became a furniture warehouse and is now the Stanley Annabelle Casino. The *Globe* opened in Primrose Hill Street in 1914; it changed ownership in 1925 and again in 1935. In 1928 it had a huge orchestral organ fitted. In 1956 it closed and was converted into the Majestic ballroom, which became the Orchid. Later it became a bingo hall, then the Tic Toc Club, then a live music venue called the Colosseum and finally the Kasbah.

The *Alexandra Picture House*, situated in Ford Street, was created from the Alexandra Coffee Tavern in 1917. The Coffee Tavern was opened in the 1890s by Councillor Samuel Allchurch. He and others had connections with Queens Road Baptist Church and were interested in the Adult School Movement, at a time when drink was a social evil. The Coffee Tavern was opened as a teetotal pub, which had a bar and even had sawdust on the floor. When Councillor Allchurch became ill he asked his nephew Charley

3

Adey to manage the tavern for him. Apart from its normal activities, it was also a centre for voluntary social work amongst the poor. Every day trades people supplied meat, bones and vegetables and this was made into soup. Anyone could have a basin filled at a cost of one penny. The tavern opened every morning at 6am and tea, coffee and cocoa along with a piece of cake, was available for the same price, for the people going to and from work. There was a high-class dining room, where professional people could have lunch for a charge of two shillings and sixpence (12.5p). The people who established the Coffee Tavern took over the canteen facilities at the Coventry Ordnance Works, at the beginning of World War One.

In 1919, the film being shown was 'The Fair Barbarian', a society drama, in which the father makes the money and the daughter spends it. Sounds familiar to things these days. The first full-length talking picture was shown in 1929. A fire damaged the interior in 1944. In 1953 the first 3D film was shown here. In 1969 the cinema closed for refurbishment and re-opened in 1970 as *Theatre One*. In 1980 it was purchased by Brian Saunders and ended up as the 'Generation Night Club', which was closed and recently put up for auction, but failed to reach its reserve.

The next generation of cinemas began in 1929, the start of the talkies. Charlie Orr and George and Harold Philpot, set up a partnership called Five Star Cinemas. They built the *Savoy* (which was the last cinema to close in their circuit), also the *Forum*, *Rex*, *Plaza* and *Ritz*. They also operated at one time or another the *Alexandra*, *Roxy* and *Brookville*. They split up in 1933 and became two separate organisations. Both went on to open many more cinemas.

The *Forum* Cinema in Walsgrave Road was a very impressive building and opened on 1st November 1934 and could seat 1,570 people. It closed on 26th May 1962 and at that time was showing Doris Day in 'Lover Come Back'. It was demolished to make way for shops and a bowling alley and had an underground car park. In 2007 it closed when the company went into liquidation.

The *Rex* Cinema in Corporation Street, was opened on 8th February 1937 by Ald. A. H. Barnacle OBE J.P. This was built in the Art Deco style and by all accounts had a lavish interior. It had two miles of carpet; the drapes were gold satin and had seating for 3,200. At the end of the pastel coloured auditorium was a screen at 31 feet wide, and was said to be the biggest in the country. Upstairs there was a restaurant and tropical birds sang in a special aviary. To filmgoers it was a palace of dreams. Its only possible rival was the *Gaumont* cinema in Jordan Well. Unfortunately, it was bombed twice in 1940. At the time of the destruction it was showing 'Gone with the Wind'. Well it did! Part of the site became the temporary Rex Market. The cinema building was not completely destroyed and was bought by Hogarth's and became a department store.

The *Savoy Cinema and Ballroom* was at 268 Radford Road and was officially opened by Captain W. F. Strickland M.P. on 2nd July 1938. It was the last cinema to be built by Harry Philpot, one of the two men who dominated the cinema circuits before the war. He was a builder by trade, as was his fellow cinema magnate Charles Orr. It could seat 1,300 and had a small Wurlitzer organ, which was bought for £2,000 (later it was sold for scrap). It was thought to have been one of the best-designed cinemas in Coventry; perhaps it would have been better if it had been built in the centre of the city. It was bombed on 14th November 1940 and was again hit by raids at Easter 1941 and it re-opened the same year in September. St. Nicholas Church, which was opposite the cinema, was flattened by a landmine in the April 1941 raid and for a short time the ballroom was used for Sunday services. Members of the Cinema Organ Society visited the *Savoy* for their final recitals on the organ. The recitals were given by well-known organists from many parts of the country and they could last for up to three hours. It was closed as a cinema in 1962 and is now a bingo club. It is still possible to see what it looked like as a cinema.

The *Standard* cinema in Tile Hill Lane opened in 1938 and became the *Godiva* in the 1960s and ran until 1976. It is now a gaming casino. I can remember going to see Bill Hayley in 'Rock Around The Clock', and rocking and rolling in the car park when the film was finished.

The *Crown* cinema was situated at 150 Far Gosford Street; it opened in 1912 and closed in 1958 when it was refurbished and became the *Paris*. It was renowned for X certificate films; these were only for people over the age of eighteen. The X rating indicated strong adult content, including sexuality, nudity, violence and profanity. The cinema finally closed in 1981.

The *Brookville* cinema at 154 Holbrooks Lane, was built in 1928 and closed in 1940 when it was bombed. It is now used by Karpet Kingdom, from the appearance of the outside you can see that it was a cinema. Bill Hockton, my friend Lynn's father- in-law, was not allowed in the services during the war, because he had a weak leg due to having polio as a child. He was assigned to do firewatching duties at Dunlop in Holbrooks Lane. The *Brookville* cinema was directly opposite the factory. On the night in 1940 when the cinema suffered damage from incendiaries, Bill was on duty. Seeing that the cinema had been hit some of the men rushed across the road to see if they could put the incendiaries out. They climbed up on to the balcony that ran across the front and were busy putting out the incendiaries when the balcony began to drop. There was a lot of shouting and the other men began to jump off, but Bill not being so nimble was left clinging to the balcony as it slowly sank to the ground. I can just imagine him shouting and carrying on at the others for leaving him there. Fortunately he was not hurt and he did keep everyone entertained with the story for years afterwards.

The *Picture Palace*, in Stoney Stanton Road, opened in 1910 and in 1940 it was completely destroyed when it was bombed. The *Carlton* cinema was situated at 574 Stoney Stanton Road, it opened in 1930 and closed down after the war. It then became a furniture business. The *Prince of Wales* cinema, 369 Stoney Stanton Road, opened in 1913 and ran until 1956. The cinema had seating for 420 people and was modernised and extended in 1951 at a cost of over £6,000. The Coventry Evening Telegraph (C.E.T.) dated 31st May 1956, wrote that the cinema was sold for £5,000 at auction and stated 'The cinema, the oldest still operating in Coventry, was bought on behalf of St. Finbarr's Hurling and Football Club, which is a Coventry Irish organisation, who hope to turn it into a social and recreational centre for Irish people. Structural alterations will be required such as levelling the sloping floor would be necessary'. It now stands empty and has been vandalised.

The *Grand Picture House* was at 511 Foleshill Road and it opened in 1908 later to become the *Regal* in 1930, this closed in 1960. The evening film shown in 1944 was 'Wuthering Heights', featuring Laurence Olivier and Merle Oberon. The cinema continued to entertain patrons through the war. Today it is used as a cash and carry store.

The *Redesdale* cinema opened in 1934 at 224 Foleshill Road and changed its name in 1952 to the *Roxy*. An article in the C.E.T. dated 11th May 1956 stated that two cinemas the *Dovedale* in Longford Road and the *Redesdale* in Foleshill Road were to be offered for sale by auction. Both of the cinemas were built and owned by Mr W.H. Bassett-Green, the man who gave the Godiva Statue to Coventry. The *Dovedale* opened in 1929 and had 914 seats and the *Redesdale* in 1934 and had seating for 1,300. They were to be offered as one lot and if they were not disposed of in that way they would then be offered in two separate lots. They were both withdrawn from the auction as they failed to meet their reserve. According to the C.E.T. dated 2nd August 1956 the *Dovedale* was sold privately and after a £10,000 modernisation programme it was to re-open later in the year as the *Ritz*. It was planned to have a 35ft wide screen and Cinemascope equipment along with new carpets and seating. Improvements would also be made to the car park. In the C.E.T. dated 9th October 1956 the *Redesdale* was sold privately, and it was expected to re-open as a club dance hall. A spokesman said 'At one stage, the possibility of turning the cinema into a skating rink was considered, but it was decided to make it into a dance hall for a private club'. It closed in the 1960s and is now a place of worship for the local Asian community.

Gaumont Cinema, now Ellen Terry building.

The *Gaumont* in Jordan Well was built in 1931 and it also housed a ballroom. I can remember queuing in the pouring rain to see the Beatles in a 'Hard Day's Night'. In 1967 it became the *Odeon*. In 1975 it had a triple screen, but in 1998 the cinema was taken over by Coventry University for its students and is now the Ellen Terry Building.

La Scala in Far Gosford Street opened in 1913 and in the 1950s it became the *Odeon*. It closed in 1963 and was destroyed by fire in 1970. Both the *Gaumont* and *La Scala* belonged to the same group and the *Gaumont* took the *Odeon* name after the original closed.

The *Empire Theatre* in Hertford Street, was opened on 30th June 1906 by the Mayor, Alderman A. H. Drinkwater, who was accompanied by Ellen Terry, the actress. It was originally built on the site of the old Corn Exchange and was partially destroyed by bombing in the Second World War. It changed its name to the ABC and was rebuilt on the same site when Hertford Street was pedestrianised. There was another change of name soon afterwards to the *Cannon*. It had enjoyed a renaissance with the other two cinemas in the city centre. I went with my friend in the early 1960s to see 'Gone with the Wind'. We queued for a very long time and the cinema was full to capacity. However, the *Cannon* could not survive and eventually closed, it is now a sports shop.

The *Opera House*, in Hales Street was built in 1889 and became the theatre home of the Coventry Repertory Company for a short time. After it was bombed in 1940, it was restored and turned into a cinema, this continued until 1961 when it was demolished and a row of shops were built on the site. In June 1944, the film was 'Fallen Sparrow' and the stars were Maureen O'Hara and John Garfield.

The *Royal Electric* cinema, situated between Matterson, Huxley and Watson and the *Opera House* was built around 1910-12, by Mr Gus Pell. It had a long narrow auditorium and seating for 165. There was a small central kiosk for ticket sales inside the vestibule. The projection box was behind the back row of seats; this was lined with sheet iron for safety reasons and the front entrance was enclosed with iron shutters, but these were open between performances. Frankie Turner bought the cinema in 1927 and changed the name to the *Royal Cinema*, but the licence was not renewed until 1931. A singer called Billy Williams was employed to sing appropriate musical numbers to the pictures. At certain matinees tea and coffee was offered to the patrons. The prices of the seats were originally threepence (1p) and sixpence (2.5p); they were later increased to fourpence (1.5p) and eightpence (3p). Films like 'Cleopatra' and 'The Battle of Waterloo' were shown and it is said that people would be queuing right back to the Hippodrome.

The *Picture House*, in Smithford Street, had a rat problem, which obviously emanated from the adjoining market, and during the film if the rats got noisy the owner would let two dogs loose to clear the cinema of them. There were strict moral codes as to what films could be shown.

In 1917 the cinema was fined ten pounds for showing an unsuitable film on a Sunday.

Some of the cinema buildings were magnificent and some of them that are used now for other purposes still bear the hallmarks of their origins. The names of the cinemas suggested glamour or American glitz. Not like the high-rise buildings, with no character that we have today. During my research I could not help but notice how many of the cinemas were destroyed during the war.

The death knell for cinemas was in the 1950s. This was possibly due to people having televisions. 1946 was a peak year for cinema attendance in Britain with 1,640 million visits, compared with 1966 when there were only seven million.

Angela Atkin

Acknowledgements
Thank you to Coventry Central Library – Local Studies for their help

Bibliography
Earlsdon Heritage Trail – Mary Montes
A Century of News – Alton Douglas
Newspaper Cuttings from the Coventry Evening Telegraph
– 1954,1956,1960,1962,1969,1982,1988,2000,2002.

The Girl Guides

Robert Baden-Powell was a distinguished Army Officer who loved the outdoor life and was particularly fond of camping. Soldiers were trained to be scouts or guides, and the motto, 'Be Prepared,' he originally gave to the South African Constabulary when he was training them, and this would become the Boy Scouts' motto. As Baden-Powell's army career was coming to a close, he started to observe the way in which boys and girls were spending their time. His own life had been a great adventure; could he not use his knowledge and experience to provide scouting for boys? He got a small group of boys together and took them camping on Brownsea Island in Poole Harbour in 1907. They loved it.

Scouting spread at a fantastic rate, of course it gave ordinary boys a chance to get out and have some adventure, at a time when few would otherwise have had any opportunity to do so. In 1908 the book *Scouting for Boys* was published and thousands of boys became Scouts. The book had another effect, the sisters of the scouts got hold of the book and they also wanted to become Scouts. They called themselves Girl Scouts, adapted the boys' uniform and managed to find ladies who were willing to become their leaders.

On 4th September 1909, only two years from the beginning of the Boy Scout movement, the first Scout rally and conference was held at the Crystal Palace, in London. The object was to show the public the aims and progress of the movement and how it had grown in that short time. When the first band of Girl Scouts appeared, Baden-Powell saw them and said, 'Who are you and what are you doing here?' Their leader, Marguerite de Beaumont, saluted and replied, 'Please sir, we are the Wolf Patrol of the Girl Scouts, and we want to do scouting like the boys.'

Baden-Powell saw no reason why the girls should be deprived of the opportunity, particularly as they had got this far on their own initiative. He invited Marguerite to meet him at his London home to discuss things and as he thought that the girls should have a different name to the boys, he chose another name from his army days – Guides. Agnes Baden-Powell, sister of Robert, wrote the first Girl Guide book *How Girls Can Help to Build up the Empire*, as she took a great interest in the movement.

In 1912 Baden-Powell met Olave St. Clair Soames; despite his being thirty-two years older than her, they quickly fell in love and were married within the year. Olave's family were country gentry; it was a very class-conscious age and in her own words she had led 'a happy, sheltered, but utterly useless existence' up to the time of her marriage. However, she loved the outdoors and rode horses, cycled, could handle a boat, played tennis and much more. She took an immediate interest in her husband's Scouting activities.

The Girl Guide movement had a rather unexciting programme at that time, as whilst it gave girls the opportunity to take their first steps towards independence, parents were worried that they might become unwomanly. However, the outbreak of the First World War was to change all that. With women taking on a greater role in the war effort, Baden-Powell received many letters urging him to do something about the Girl Guides. He obtained a Charter of Incorporation and set up a new committee of younger women, who commenced the organisation of Guiding along Scout lines. There would be a Commissioner for each county, and in March 1916 Olave became County Commissioner for Sussex. There were always plenty of girls, but the problem was finding leaders. In October 1916 the Commissioners held their first conference at Matlock and there were twenty-six leaders. Olave was elected Chief Commissioner at the meeting and in February 1918 she was made Chief Guide.

Both Scouts and Guides continued to grow apace. The Baden-Powells became worldwide celebrities and travelled to America, Canada, India and most countries in Europe. In May 1932 there was a Service of Thanks giving in St. Paul's Cathedral to mark the coming of age year of Guiding, at which 5,300 Guides renewed their Promise. Princess Mary was present, as she had become Guide President in 1920. Indeed, the female members of the Royal family have all joined the Guides since it became an established movement.

In 1922 Princess Mary married the Earl of Harewood. All Guide members by the name of Mary in the empire, contributed to a wedding present. At this time, Mrs Archbold Sanderson offered to the Guides, a property, called 'Foxlease' near Lyndhurst in the New Forest. It would make an ideal training centre for Guiders, but to convert and equip it and

11

then maintain the house and grounds would be very costly. Princess Mary offered half of the 'Mary's' money, plus the fees for viewing her wedding presents and 'Foxlease' became a viable proposition. In 1931 an American woman, Mrs. Storrow, gave a chalet at Adelboden in Switzerland to the Guides, as an international skiing and training centre.

The 7th World Guide Conference was held at Katowice in Poland in 1932. A Belgian Guider suggested that one day in each year should be set apart to think of each other in terms of love and friendship. A practical suggestion was added, that every Guide should contribute 'A penny for your thoughts' to World Association funds. February 22nd, the birthday of both Robert and Olave Baden-Powell, was chosen. In 1933 £520.12s.6d was contributed and in 1970/71 the sum increased to £35,346.

Camping quickly became a very important part of Guiding and detailed instructions were contained in the book *Campcraft for Girl Guides*, published in the 1920s. This makes very interesting reading; it contains instructions on the choice of camp site, pitching tents, digging a latrine, different types of camp fire for cooking and a lot more. A suggested menu is given, at a cost of 8s (40p) per Guide for one week. Should an improved breakfast be wanted, it would cost an additional 1s 3d (6p), bringing it to the grand total of 9s 3d (46p) for the week. The kit list for each Guide reads thus; 1 palliasse cover (straw will be provided), 2 blankets, 1 pillowcase, 1 bath and 2 face towels, 1 glass cloth, 1 warm jumper, 1 extra skirt, 1 overcoat or waterproof, 3 pairs black stockings, 1 pair sandshoes, 2 pairs strong boots or shoes, 1 pair dark blue knickers, 1 change underclothes, 1 pair warm pyjamas, 1 overall or apron, Guide uniform, camp overall, handkerchief, hair, nail and tooth brushes, hair comb, nail scissors, soap and flannel, tooth powder, 2 enamel plates, 1 mug, 1 bowl, 1 knife, fork, dessert and teaspoon, notebook and pencil, signalling flag (if required) and a small ball of string.

Guiding in Coventry nowadays is split into two divisions – Coventry North and Coventry South. There is a shortage of leaders (all volunteers of course) although this is a modern trend in many organisations. The number of Guides has declined in recent years and the older girls can now join the Scouts, which they probably find more exciting and there are many other interests and holidays available. So it is currently mainly the very young girls' groups, Rainbows and Brownies. Each group has a weekly meeting, often held

Rosemary Eley and some of the Rainbows.

in a church hall or sometimes a schoolroom, where they play games, but they have to obey the instructions and are encouraged to take an interest in the world around them. For instance a pack of Brownies have recently collected items to make up school packs for African children who cannot attend school without pens, pencils, notebooks, etc. The girls all try to collect as many badges as they can; these are available for all sorts of achievements such as, art, cookery, entertaining by singing, dancing or playing a musical instrument, swimming and other sports.

The main aim of Guiding is 'To help every girl to attain the highest development of which she is capable.' The promise, which the girls make when they are enrolled, has been adapted somewhat over the years. The Brownie version, which commenced in 1994, is 'I promise that I will do my best to love my God, to serve the Queen and my country, to help other people and to keep the Brownie Guide law.' The uniform worn by the girls has also changed over the years, so that they do not feel old-fashioned. They do still camp, but on sites with more adequate facilities than in the days of *Campcraft for Girl Guides*. Coventry South has its own site at Fillongley, with Porta-Cabin type accommodation.

I will finish on a personal note. Some thirty years ago, whilst my daughter was in Guiding, the Coventry South Commissioner wanted to set up some Local Association (later known as Friends of Guiding) groups amongst the girls' mothers. A meeting was arranged in Copsewood district and our group began. We organised events such as Brownie discos, fun nights and so forth, any profit made being available for extra equipment. We also undertook badge testing. We were asked to send a representative to join the Headquarters Committee, and I was asked to do this. Eventually, I became treasurer for Headquarters. The Friends of Guiding group lasted for

13

a number of years, by which time all our daughters had left and gone away to university or for work and as no new mothers had joined us, we decided that the group must finish. However, I remained as Headquarters treasurer for several years after this. The Coventry South Headquarters is a Victorian house in Grosvenor Road. The Guide leaders use the rooms for meetings, but they are also let them to others, such as the University of the Third Age (U3A), Coventry Scrabble club and others. The car park is let to local office workers and the upstairs rooms are let to Coventry University students. The income enables us to keep the house in good repair. Eventually it was time for our group to move on, but we had all tried to do our share for Guiding and I still have good friends as a result.

Kathleen Barker

Acknowledgements

I would like to say many thanks to Rosemary Eley, who has lent to me the books, which have enabled me to write this article.

The Women's Institute

Is it all Jam and Jerusalem? Or as it states on the website 'A modern voice for today's woman?' The Women's Institute (WI) was originally set up in Canada at the end of the nineteenth century for the wives of the members of the Farmers' Institute. The idea travelled across the Atlantic, where the first meeting took place in Anglesey, North Wales in 1915. As Europe was in the throes of the First World War, causing severe hardship and destruction, there was even greater demand for food. Rural communities needed revitalising and as so many men were heading for military service on the Continent, women were in great demand to work on the land, as well as in factories in the cities. The Women's Land Army also came into being during this period in our history.

The WI is now the largest organisation for women in the United Kingdom. Originally a rural institution, dealing with country matters, it now has many groups based within towns and cities across the country. In 2005 it celebrated its 90th birthday and is still going strong. There are now around 205,000 members in 6,500 WIs in the country. Within the West Midlands there are 45 institutes, some meeting in the morning, some in the afternoon and others in the evening. The WI states that it has a clear role to provide women with a range of educational opportunities, to learn and build upon new skills, to have a voice and campaign on issues that matter to them.

Eastern Green WI was established around 1946. The area was mainly rural at that time, with the beginnings of modern housing between the old cottages in the village and around Alspath Lane and Eastern Green Road. Since then the urban spread of Coventry has changed the nature of the community. This urbanisation has affected the outlook of the local WI, for instead of being concerned with food production and making jam, cakes and growing food to sell at markets, the ethos has changed to concerns about the environment and other modern issues.

The chance to learn new skills and develop interests and education are available to members of the WI through courses organised at Denman College in Abingdon, Oxfordshire. It was named after the first Chairman of the Federation of Women's Institutes, Lady Denman. There is a wide range of courses on offer, from IT, cookery, crafts, horticulture and much more.

The courses are residential and each federation is responsible for furnishing a bedroom within the college, to hotel standard, and creating the ambiance of that region, with books and information about the area. The tutors who teach at the college are of the highest quality.

Eastern Green is part of the West Midlands Federation and meet at the Village Hall on the first Wednesday of every month in the evening, with a speaker or demonstration arranged for their entertainment and education. Members can attend county and national events when they arise. As the WI is a charity, they do not raise money for other charities, but they do support them by making items to send to those who are in the greatest need. They knit and crochet blankets that are sent to African countries and make baby clothes for the premature babies at University Hospital, Walsgrave. Individual members arrange coffee mornings in their own homes with sales of work, bring and buy stalls or raffles to raise money for the charity of choice, of the hostess. In this way the recipients of donations are very varied from Air Ambulance to Global Care, Cancer Research and others.

The current president, Janet Owen, who has filled this office for the past eight years, believes in maintaining the traditions of the WI whilst keeping a modern focus. Janet became a member of the local WI after the death of her husband fourteen years ago. A friend of hers told her about the group and encouraged her to give it a try. She joined because she needed company, to make new friends and have fun. She definitely achieved all of these aims and has never regretted becoming part of Eastern Green WI. When she joined there were 29 members, but numbers have increased to 40.

Janet believes that the main role and aims of the WI are similar to those that were in place when it was founded, bringing the community together by focusing on particular issues. In the early days it was the need to produce more food during wartime and helping women in rural communities to develop their skills to the benefit of their families and the local area. Times have changed, but there are still issues that concern WI members, although they probably have a wider scope and are not just local.

The group arranges outings for its members to visit places of interest. Janet mentioned a few of those visited recently. There was a visit to Highgrove, the home of the Prince of Wales in 2008. Another place that impressed many of the members was the National Arboretum at Alrewas in Staffordshire.

This is an ongoing development of land to commemorate members of the armed forces and auxiliary services, who were involved in not only the two World Wars, but also conflicts that have taken place since. There are no grave stones in uniform rows, such as those managed by the War Graves Commission on the Continent, but monuments to service regiments, ARP, Home Guard, ATS, WRNS, the Fire Service, Police, Trefoil, the WI and many more.

One of the projects mentioned by Janet was the decision to celebrate the millennium by knitting 2000 teddies. The group began this mammoth project in November 1998 and had already knitted 1000 by April 1999. Many more teddies went on to be knitted until they had reached 2,500. They were donated to 'Feed the Children' for distribution to children in many countries, where the need was felt to be greatest. This event was picked up by the BBC Midlands Today and Shefali Oza and a camera crew

L-R Shefali Oza, Beryl Allen, Janet Owen and Marion Vines

came. They took film footage and photographs of WI members surrounded by knitted teddies. It was a fantastic achievement and is still continuing to this day, bringing a lot of happiness to children around the world who have very little or nothing of their own.

Beryl Allen has been a member of Eastern Green WI for 47 years. Born in Birmingham, she came to Coventry as a young mother of two small children. She thought she would never settle, separated from her family back in Birmingham. A neighbour suggested that she should join the local WI to meet people and get involved in the community. She had never even heard of the WI, being very much a town dweller. When her neighbour mentioned institute, she thought it must be something to do with a hospital. However, she decided to go and try it out.

There were very few young women there and Beryl did wonder if it was for her. However, she met and became friends with another young member,

Beryl Lee. Her mother was a founder member and took her daughter along with her after a few years. Beryl Lee has been a member for 60 years, of which she has spent 50 years in various positions on the committee. At present she holds the office of Secretary and is very much appreciated by the membership of Eastern Green WI.

Beryl Allen soon settled into the routine and came to appreciate just what a wonderful organisation the WI is. She says that all the craft skills that she possesses now, and she has many, are due to the WI. She has attended courses at Denman College on many occasions and thoroughly enjoyed it. She has met and made numerous friends over the years and is very well known in Eastern Green. She has held most of the offices in the WI during that time.

The two Beryls have seen changes over their long years of membership and the 'Jam and Jerusalem' image has been somewhat diluted. They do still sing Jerusalem at the beginning of their meetings as it is a very uplifting hymn and gets them off to a good start. Eastern Green does not involve itself in produce markets, but many members are skilled jam and cake makers. The WI would like to encourage more young women to join, but in today's economic climate many women, even with young children, have to work. There is still a preponderance of older women, but at least they look and often feel more youthful and energetic than women did in the past.

The WI has had to adapt and move with the times to maintain their membership. Some organisations have fallen by the wayside through lack of support, but the WI is still going strong 94 years on. Like other groups they sometimes have trouble filling the positions on the committee, but without those officers it would not exist. It is an institute that many of us would like to see continue for a very long time.

Ali McGarry and Lynn Hockton

Acknowledgements
Thank you to Janet Owen and Beryl Allen for sharing their memories of the WI with us.
Historical information from the WI website.

G E C Ballroom

The General Electric Company (GEC) transferred its Peel Conner factory from Manchester to Coventry in 1918. The management, like many of the day, put a high priority on the welfare and social activities of its employees. It encouraged its staff to participate in organised sports and social events, which proved very popular with the workforce. It was due to the success of the sports and social club that the GEC built the self contained units, comprising of a social club, large canteen and ballroom.

Built in 1920 the ballroom was a very majestic building, from a high ceiling, hung two huge glitter balls. The dance floor could compete with any in the country, being of sprung Canadian spruce. In the centre stood a tiered fountain, which was sadly sacrificed during the war for badly needed scrap metal. The stage was equipped with all the sophistications of the day. The whole of the electrics was refined to a professional standard by the chief electrician, a Bob Camp, who was once employed by the Strand Theatre in London.

In the early days the ballroom was affectionately known as Conner's and hosted Saturday night dances with the Rhythmics dance band, which played regularly until 1925. They were followed by the Gaiety dance band, which

The Gaiety Band 1927.

played at dances on Saturday and Wednesday nights. Wednesday became known as the tanner hop, a reference to the admission price, which was 6d (2.5p) Saturday nights cost a shilling (5p). The Gaiety band left in 1937 and was succeeded by Billy Monk and his band, which played regularly on Wednesday night and occasionally Mondays. Vincent Ladrock and Tony Liddell played on alternate Saturdays until 1939 when Billy Monk took over permanently, playing at all dances.

During the war the BBC home service broadcast a lunchtime variety programme called Workers Playtime. It was a huge boost to the morale of Coventry's workers when this programme was broadcast from the GEC ballroom on three separate occasions.

All attendance records were broken on VE (Victory in Europe) Day as the crowds that night filled the ballroom to bursting point, causing dancers to overflow into the adjacent canteen. It was reported that 1,800 patrons celebrated in the ballroom that night. The atmosphere must have been electric.

Billy Monk retired in 1956 but the band continued to play under Ces Jeffs until 1958 when they decided to call it a day because the big band had become outdated. The culprit for this sad demise was the invasion of pop music and the electric guitar, which changed the music and dance scene. Saturday night dances continued and were brought up to date by groups such as the Eclipse Combo and the Lloyd Scott Sound. The Old-Time dances with the Valeta, Polka and Military Two-Step still proved popular, however, and continued on Monday nights from the 1950s until the 1970s.

For people who wanted to take up dancing or improve their technique, national champions Les Knight and his wife held lessons every Tuesday night, and Friday was reserved for dinner dances, which the works department's sports section and social club took great advantage of. Social club events included the annual Miss GEC, Easter Bonnet and New Years Eve dance. Many evening dress dances were held for firms such as the Law Society, British Legion Ceremony of Remembrance and the British Medical Association.

Dancing was not the only pastime for which the ballroom was used. The social club had an amateur dramatics society, which presented a spring and autumn play of a high standard. The Variety Society produced a

GEC Ballroom with the newly installed lighting system, November 1937

pantomime each Christmas, which escalated from three to six nights due to popular demand. Mac Crook wrote and produced the pantomime (plus seven spring shows) from 1944 to 1964 after which, George Nottingham took up the reins and continued the tradition.

There must be thousands of Coventry citizens who remember the annual children's Christmas party, which was held in the ballroom. At its peak during the 1960s, 300 children aged five to ten were entertained every night over a period of six nights. Another organised function arranged in the ballroom was the reunion for retired personnel, when over a period of four nights, 400 to 500 senior citizens were entertained each night.

A unique annual gathering was organised by the GEC Rugby Club, known as the 'Hot Pot.' The event was brought down from Lancashire by the President of the club Alderman W H Malcolm, Managing Director of GEC and Mayor of Coventry. Both he and his catch phrase 'Now Bohoooys' was respected by all. At one function 640 patrons representing all Rugby clubs in the Warwickshire area witnessed the presentation of Warwickshire caps and the evening was described by the then President of the Rugby Football Union, W C Ramsey, as 'The largest social gathering of Rugby footballers anytime, anywhere.'

So many artists performed and events took place in the GEC ballroom that some are bound to be overlooked, but two that should be remembered are: the fourteen piece GEC orchestra that gave an annual week-long concert under the direction of Arthur Clark and soloist Tommie Bell who gave lunchtime concerts on the Hammond organ, which was a permanent fixture within the dance hall.

Jean Appleton

Jean experienced first hand the joys of the GEC ballroom in the early 1950s. At that time dances were held three times weekly, Monday, Wednesday and Thursday. She loved dancing and would go, as often as she could, with a friend whom she met while working at the General Post Office. There were a few good dance halls in Coventry, but as her friend's father worked at the GEC and lived on the company's housing estate it probably influenced the choice of venue.

'I went dancing regularly on Monday nights, although it was not the best night because we had to dance to records. If there were not enough males to partner us, girls danced together. It was still an enjoyable evening. By this time I had begun nurse training at Coventry and Warwickshire Hospital, which, of course, involved shift working including spells of night duty. To go dancing was a real treat and rarity for me. As night duty began at 10.30pm I could leave the dance at ten o'clock and be at the hospital in time to change into my uniform to go on duty.

I especially looked forward to the Saturday night dance, which I only managed to attend when working on the early, day shift. This began at 7.30am so I did not always have the prospect of a lie in the following morning, but it didn't worry me. Billy Monk's band played regularly and drew in the crowd. Nothing compensates for dancing to a live band, so there was never a shortage of partners of the opposite sex. I could really let myself go and dance the night away. I loved to dance the *foxtrot*, *waltz* and the *quickstep*, which was my particular favourite. The *tango* was difficult, but there was an easier version, the *square tango*.

All the boys wore jackets and ties, while the girls wore attractive dresses or skirts with a fancy blouse. I had a dirndl skirt, which was fashionable at the time. It had gathers all round from a deep waistband like Tyrolean skirts. With it I wore a white sleeveless blouse bordered with lace. I always seemed to have an especially good time when wearing this outfit.

The dance hall was used for many different, private functions. It was the venue for a ball for the Nurses of Coventry and Warwickshire Hospital. The men all wore evening dress. There was a good turn out of medical staff from consultants to junior housemen and those from several departments such as radiographers and technicians. The nurses, of course, were in attractive, long dresses. They had asked for invitations to be sent to anyone they wished to take. A few of the nurses, including me, were working on nights. However, the nurses working the late day duty offered to stay until midnight to enable us to attend the dance.

The GEC had a drama company, which had a very good reputation. Besides producing plays they put on a pantomime at Christmas. This was very popular and tickets were soon sold out. I had a sister-in-law who worked at the company so she suggested I take her daughter, my niece, to a performance. The hall was full and the entertainment was thoroughly enjoyed by the audience.

I had many good times at the GEC ballroom, when I was young and single, and felt very sad when I learned that it was closing. So many memories came to my mind, including the occasion when my friend first met the man who later became her husband. Although it is over fifty years since we were two carefree young friends just enjoying ourselves on a Saturday night, sometimes it seems like only yesterday.'

Ann Waugh

The GEC ballroom was a revelation to me at the age of sixteen years. I wanted to learn ballroom dancing and my friend suggested we go along to the GEC on a Monday night. It was quite cheap as we would only be dancing to records and there was an instructor called Les Knight. He demonstrated with his wife, Cynthia, they were very professional and often took part in competitions.

There were usually 25-30 young people there and we had to stand at the side while Les showed us the steps. He then selected a partner, quite often me, as I was quite tall and he was very tall. I used to be petrified, especially as he used to hold me very close and in a loud voice say, 'In ballroom dancing, you lead with the thighs.' You can imagine the comments I got when we had general dancing after the lesson!

The ballroom was beautiful, very large, with a stage at one end where the band played and seats on both sides of the ballroom. At the other end there was a large space underneath the balcony. In the centre of the ceiling was a huge glitter ball, which rotated for the dancers. Very few people sat on the seats, especially me, as being tall, it was very embarrassing if, when asked to dance, you towered above the young lad, so most people stood underneath the balcony.

After paying your money at the door, you went into the works canteen where you changed into your dancing shoes. I had bought mine on a trip to London and they were made of Perspex with black bows. Our outdoor shoes and coats were given to the attendant. You could buy soft drinks from the canteen, but no alcohol. There was a bar upstairs in the Social Club and we used to look forward to closing time at 10.30pm when the number of young men wanting to dance with the girls doubled!

On Wednesday and Saturday evenings, there was dancing to the resident band, Billy Monk, accompanied by his two singers, Rita and Alan. These dances were very well attended, especially Saturday when we often had to queue to get in. If the Coventry Bees were riding at Brandon, people used to come straight from the stadium to dance. I remember on one occasion there were too many people, so they closed the doors and I had to return home. I can still remember the disappointment I felt. Despite the large numbers there was very little trouble. They were very strict about the rule of 'no jiving' except in the five-minute bebop session when the floor was packed. My favourite dance was the quickstep to *American Patrol*.

I always used to cycle to the dances and leave my bike in the bike sheds, no need to lock them up in those days. As I lived fairly close it was not too tiring after dancing all night. However, my friend lived in Keresley so she had a four-mile ride there and back, but we loved the dancing and it was a way of meeting people.

There were sometimes evenings with famous bands, such as Jack Parnell and his band, but these were few as it tended to be the Arden Ballroom in Bedworth where most of the big bands appeared. I remember seeing Ted Heath and his band in Bedworth, but there was no room to dance! The GEC was also used for Pantomime and other shows. It was a great disappointment to me when the ballroom closed, as I had to travel into town to the Rialto and the Locarno to do my dancing

Last Dance at the GEC Ballroom

In the 1970s as people's pastimes had changed and many of the old dance halls and cinemas had been turned into bingo halls, tombola was introduced in the ballroom on Thursday and Sunday nights and quickly became popular. Once again the ballroom was changing with the times and it continued to do so throughout the eighties.

In 1992 an article appeared in the Coventry Evening Telegraph, with the title of 'Last Waltz looms for a ballroom of memories.' This was a very appropriate title when considering the closing speech made in the ballroom by Trustee Alan Johnson who said, 'They can blow this ballroom to kingdom come, but they cannot take away the associated memories which will last for many generations.'

The final dance in the ballroom saw many familiar faces among the 380 patrons, each with their own memories of the happy times they had spent in the ballroom. It was sadly the end of an era and for some people, a part of their lives would go forever along with the ballroom. There must have been many eyes that held a silent tear that night but nevertheless in a very fitting tradition they gave the ballroom a resounding send off.

Christine Marsh

Acknowledgements

I would like to thank Alan Johnson, Jean Appleton and Ann Waugh for their contribution to this article.

Thank you to Andrew Mealey, at Coventry Archives, for permission to reproduce the photographs of the GEC Ballroom and Gaiety Band from *The Loudspeaker* magazine.

The Women's League of Health and Beauty

The League was founded by Mollie Bagot Stack, the daughter of a doctor. Having suffered rheumatic fever in her teens she became very interested in exercise as a means of regaining her health. Training at the Conn Institute in London, Mollie was taught the techniques of stretching exercises, of balance and poise to improve posture and health. She went on to teach the techniques to others.

In 1912 Mollie married Hugh, an officer in the Gurkha Regiment and went with him to India. There she admired the way the Indian women seemed to have a natural grace and poise and joined classes to learn techniques of yoga and relaxation. She developed a system of exercise combining the best of eastern and western ideas. In 1914 when the First World War started, the regiment was sent to the Western Front and tragically Hugh was killed. During that year Mollie had a daughter, Prunella and she was left to bring her up alone. Needing an income to support her daughter and herself, she resumed teaching once peace was declared.

She taught children, including her daughter, in her own home. Two sisters also took part in her classes, Peggy and Joan St. Lo, and it was the young Peggy's leaping figure, which became the logo of the Women's League of Health and Beauty. Very soon her classes became so popular with women and girls that Mollie set up a Health School in London in 1925 for exercise and dance. Her aim was to attract women and girls from all walks of life to think about exercise for their health and wellbeing. This was her philosophy of life and what inspired the motto of the League when it started – Movement is Life. Within three months of its foundation in 1930, numbers had reached 1,000, which increased to 47,000 in 1934 and 100,000 by 1936. It spread to centres all over the country and abroad during that time. Sadly Mollie had died of cancer in 1935 just as her brainchild was coming to fruition. However, her daughter took over, being a fully qualified teacher from the age of sixteen and moulded the League into a highly popular institution. Public displays were put on at Hyde Park in London and large regional parks around the country. Wembley stadium was also used to show synchronized exercise routines and large groups came from other countries to take part. The demonstrations at the Albert Hall became famous after the Second World War.

Fashions of the 1930s were slim fitting and often cut on the bias, to flow around the figure; a very flattering style on a slim figure, but not attractive on a plump shape. Young women wanted to emulate the film stars and look glamorous and this was the incentive for some to join in the exercise programmes. Most places of work practiced a marriage bar, before the Second World War, often leaving wives bored at home if they did not have young children, or the children attended school. This was another reason to join in and meet friends as well as becoming fit.

Daphne Plummer joined the League in the early 1970s. She was a member of the Monday Club, which met at St. Barbara's Church in Earlsdon, Coventry, and also attended its keep-fit class on Wednesdays. Some of the women who took part in these classes also belonged to the Women's League of Health and Beauty. One of the members, Jean Ridgeway, persuaded Daphne and a couple of other friends to join her and give it a try. The class was held on a Tuesday afternoon at Sibree Hall and the group of friends met up as they walked through Earlsdon, across the railway bridge near Spencer Park and into the city centre. After carrying out the exercise programme they retraced their steps to Earlsdon.

They all enjoyed the exercises and for some there was the bonus of a big loss of inches around the waist. A friend, who cooked the cheap meals provided by the Congregational Church in Warwick Road, came into the exercise classes when she had finished her shift. She only had to walk around the back of the church to Sibree Hall, situated just to the rear. She lost six inches off her waist and was so thrilled that she was hooked.

There were strict rules about the distance between classes, to prevent them being too thinly spread and therefore unviable. A teacher usually set up a group near the centre of the town or city and members were drawn in. The rules stated that a class could not be set up within six miles of another established group. The class at Sibree Hall was run by Margaret Sharpe, who ran her main class at Stoke Park School on Tuesday evening. She ran another group in Meriden on Thursday mornings and several of those members also went to her evening class in Stoke Park. There were others in Kenilworth, Warwick and Leamington Spa and no doubt many more in other centres around Warwickshire. Margaret Sharpe was a very good instructor, dedicated to the exercise programme. She was very active running different classes and organised rallies in the area too. She is still running classes in Kenilworth. Daphne's group had around forty members at any one time. It was common for members to attend two classes each week and Daphne was no exception. Eventually she learned to drive and this made it easier to attend the evening and out of town classes.

The uniform of white silk blouse and black satin knickers had been phased out by the time Daphne joined, as the material became difficult to source. It was replaced by the new style uniform, which looked the same, but was in fact a Lycra leotard with black lower section and white top half, zipped up the front. It bore the logo of the leaping Peggy St. Lo on the lower edge. For displays they often had to buy a different leotard and later leggings. Daphne had several, a black one with blue inset pieces around the neck and a black one with bright green leggings. This latter outfit was not an official one. The official costume did become very expensive, but if you took part in a display it was compulsory to have the official uniform. Rival companies began producing costumes much more cheaply and many members started buying them for the exercise classes, although they did not have the logo on. It was possible to buy woven badges to sew on, but of course this was not acceptable for a display.

The exercise programme concentrated on stretching. They used clubs for swinging and hoops and balls for balance and co-ordination. There were lots of floor exercises too, stretching the legs and arms in time to music. A lot of ballet movements were contained within the exercises. They always exercised in bare feet, and it was possible to cut the feet off tights, but eventually footless tights were manufactured to cater for this market. They were obtainable from ballet-supplies shops, although they became more widely available

Display at The Town and Country Festival, Stoneleigh 1980

as they became popular. The public displays of synchronized exercise looked spectacular. In the 1950s and 60s displays at the Albert Hall were televised and the precision programmes were amazing to watch. Daphne took part in the 1975 display on the 45th anniversary of the foundation of the League. They went by coach to London and some stayed overnight in a hotel, although others, including Daphne, returned that night. They met up with other members from different parts of the country and abroad. It was very exciting, but also quite exhausting.

Daphne remembers seeing a demonstration of ball exercises given by a German woman at Wheatley Street School once. She used the ball to great effect, with perfect balance and poise, she was able to control the ball and make the exercise look easy. Daphne and others tried to copy her techniques afterwards and found it was not as easy as she made it appear.

For decades the exercises were accompanied by a pianist, but in more recent years the use of music tapes has taken over. Daphne considers that the pianist is always preferable to tapes, as she can adapt quickly to the situation as she interprets it. If the pace needs to be quickened, then her response is immediate, that is not possible with tape. However, the cost has to be considered. A pianist has to be paid for her time and skill, whereas once equipment is purchased tape will go on until it is no longer required. Even if the tape breaks it is cheap to replace.

Daphne remained in the League for between thirteen and fifteen years and enjoyed it very much. She was always interested in exercise and belonged to the Keep Fit Association before that, as she had a sedentary job she felt she needed that activity. In the mid 1980s she formed a singing group with two friends Liz and Marcia. The most convenient time for them to meet was a Thursday and it clashed with the League's classes. One had to give and it was the exercise classes that she dropped in favour of the singing group. She did not abandon her keep-fit programme, however, she joined a group in Jubilee Crescent. By then leotards and leggings were widely available and very cheap from some of the bargain shops in town.

The Women's League of Health and Beauty have adapted to the needs of women as times have changed. They have changed the name to the Fitness League in more recent times, which has a more modern appeal. It is partly funded by Sport England and Sport Scotland. A class fee is paid to the teacher at each session and an annual fee goes direct to head office to pay for the services they provide. The League is just as relevant now as it always was, if not more so. With the growing incidence of obesity in adults and children, the need for more exercise is paramount. Let us hope that it continues for many more years to come.

Lynn Hockton

Acknowledgements

Thank you to Daphne Plummer for sharing her memories of the League and even demonstrating some of the exercises. She is still very fit.
The Fitness League's website for information on Mollie Bagot Stack.

Coventry Repertory Company

One of the heavy bombing raids on Coventry towards the end of 1940 brought an end to an era of entertainment that had lasted almost ten years. Despite the relatively short period of its existence the Coventry Repertory Company (the Rep) was a very popular institution in the city.

The Rep was founded in 1931 and based at the Opera House in Hales Street. The theatre was an imposing building sandwiched between the Old Grammar School and Matterson, Huxley & Watson. It was opened in 1889 and dwarfed the buildings either side. It was four storeys high with a suggestion of Dutch gabling about the roof. At the time of its opening the theatre was owned and managed by W. Bennett, who was succeeded by H.G. Dudley Bennett in 1912. By the time the Rep were producing plays at the Opera House, Mrs H.G. Dudley Bennett was the licensee and Walter D. Nicoll the Manager.

The Rep was very successful because it gave the audience what it wanted. Generally the plays put on were light entertainment by authors like George Bernard Shaw, Ivor Novello, Somerset Maugham, Noel Coward, J.M. Barrie and many more who are no longer so well known as

The Opera House

they were in the 1930s. They were not averse to putting on plays by women too, such as *Autumn Crocus* by Dodie Smith, although she did write under the pseudonym of C.L. Anthony. There was a core of actors who seemed to appear in almost every play in the early days, although the cast became more varied as the years went by and there were some who became famous in later years. The very first play to be produced, in the week commencing 6th April 1931, was called *Aren't We All* by Frederick Lonsdale and starred

Paul Nelson, Howieson Culff (also producer), Florence Leclercq and Jean Parrington.

The old programmes are a mine of information about the play of the week, the one being staged the following week and included photographs of the actors taking part. As the company became more established, small articles appeared about theatre personalities and a review of productions being staged at other repertory theatres around the country. The advertisements are fascinating and the revenue from them obviously contributed towards the cost of printing the programme. One of the most prolific advertisers was Anslows, the furniture store in High Street. They must have loaned furniture for the stage sets too, as they are acknowledged in the text. Others were thanked such as The Geisha Café, for their table appointment and Abdulla who supplied the cigarettes. Other advertisers included A. Pargetter & Son, the funeral directors, still going strong today, and Hogarth, a department store on Foleshill Road.

The auditorium was made up of the stalls, the circle and an upper circle. There was a graduated scale of charges for the seats, as in any theatre. In 1934 the Orchestra Stalls were 2s.5d (12p), Circle 1s.6d (7.5p), Pit 1s (5p), Balcony 9d (4p) and Gallery 5d (2p). Prices remained almost static throughout the years. If you made a block booking the prices were reduced by a few pence. There were two houses nightly commencing at 6.30pm and 8.50pm. The second house seems to be a late start, but to assist its audience the late bus timetables were published in the programme for them to plan their journey home. It all appears to have been organised very well, with the bus companies timing their last departures to accommodate the audience, not only of the Opera House, but other late night entertainment. For the more opulent members of the audience there was a large car park at the rear of the theatre.

The programme dated 23rd April 1934 shows that the play that week was *The Rose Without A Thorn* by Clifford Bax. It had the usual layout of articles and advertising, but in addition it informed the reader that on 7th May they would be recording a short play called *Afternoon* by Philip Johnson. The BBC Midland Region would be broadcasting it that day on the radio at 8.30pm, but it would not interfere with the normal performance.

The theatre management staged regular art shows in the foyer. During the week of 4th June 1934 there was a one-man show by J.H. Norman NSA, offering his paintings for sale at five guineas each. When the play *England Expects* by Edgar Middleton was staged, there was a display of valuable Admiral Lord Nelson relics in the vestibule. On another occasion there was a visit from the famous novelist, Ian Hay, whose plays they staged periodically. It was obviously quite a coup to have persuaded him to attend.

A group of enthusiastic supporters of the Rep formed a club called the Coventry Repertory Circle. They had regular meetings and arranged speakers. They held an annual dance for family and friends of Circle members. In 1935, three hundred people attended such an occasion at St. John's Hall, Holyhead Road. Charles Shadwell and his Orchestra from the Hippodrome played for their entertainment.

During the period when the Rep was using the Opera House, there was a fire under the stage, which damaged equipment and props stored there. A passing policeman doing his rounds at 1.20am discovered the fire. He saw smoke coming from a window and called the Fire Brigade. As the Fire Station was situated at the other end of Hales Street, they arrived promptly to deal with the emergency. There was quite extensive water damage at the front of house, but the impression was given that the show would go on. There appears to have been no explanation for the fire, but with hindsight it could have been a wiring fault or a dropped cigarette end, as so many people smoked at the time and little thought was given to health and safety issues.

It is coming up to 78 years since the Rep commenced its life at the Opera House and there is a very limited number of people who actually remember being part of the audience in the 1930s. Kath Deacon, aged 90, first went to a performance when she was about 15 or 16, around 1933-4. She went every week afterwards with her parents, older sister and her sister's friend, Marjorie. Her mother was in charge of collecting the money and booking the tickets for them all. By making a block booking of five seats, she was able to get a reduction of 3d (1p) on every seat, making the cost 1s.3d (6p) instead of 1s.6d (7.5p). Her family always reserved the same seats, second row from the front in the Circle.

As they regularly went to the first performance on a Saturday night, it was always a rush to have a meal and get a bus or tram to the theatre for 6.30pm. It was nearly always a full house and they sat enthralled by the play for the next couple of hours. She recalls a very varied mixture of plays, changing the programme every week. She was very keen on collecting the autographs of the many stars and supporting actors that she saw there. They were not arrogant or brusque when asked for an autograph, but pleasant and obliging. She even went to the Stage Door, at the side of the building, to catch the actors going in to the theatre and sometimes as they came through the foyer. A friend from Kath's church, called Bobby Bright, was a landlady to some of the actors who visited the theatre.

Kath believes that there was nowhere in Coventry like the Opera House at the time. It was very well decorated, with gold mouldings and plush red seating. There was a bar there and a place to buy soft drinks, but she was more interested in buying an ice cream during the interval, from the usherette with her tray of goodies. All the staff members, she recalled, seemed to be quite young. Apart from these weekly trips to the Opera House, her only other source of entertainment was to go dancing at her local church hall. She worked as a comptometer operator at the Council House after completing a training course, which cost her parents 12 guineas (£12.60).

Like Kath, Dorothy Parker took advantage of the block booking system to save a little money when she went with a group of friends to the Opera House for the Rep performances. She thinks her first visit was made around 1932, when she was aged 19, as she had just started to put her hair up. She went regularly each week right up until the war. Some of the actors she particularly remembered seeing were Vivien Leigh and Ann Casson. In her opinion, the decorations at the theatre had become jaded by the beginning of the war and were badly in need of money spending on improvements.

Sheila MacDonald is another Coventry resident who remembers attending the theatre to see plays put on by the Rep. She went every week and saw Phyllis Calvert, Richard Hurndall and June Duprez, all well-known actors. June Duprez went on to work in Hollywood and starred in *The Thief of Bagdad* made by Alexander Korda. Sheila was still at school when she started going to the theatre with her mother. She attended Kings High School for girls in Warwick and returned to Coventry by bus in the late afternoon. Her mother would take her for something to eat before heading for the theatre in time for the first house at 6.30pm. They always sat in the circle during the performance, but if they wanted the cheaper seats they had to queue at the back entrance. One play Sheila remembers vividly is *Journey's End* by R.C. Sherriff about the First World War. This illustrates that it was not only comedy and light entertainment that was staged there, as this is a rather sombre, thought-provoking play. The theatre opened all year round, unlike some that closed during the summer or put on a different programme.

Megan Saxelby was lucky enough to visit the theatre regularly for free. She lived with her parents in Radford, where one of her neighbours, Mrs. Causer, worked at the Opera House Box Office. Not only that, she let rooms to some of the actors performing with the Rep. She was given complimentary tickets every week, and as she did not want to use them herself she gave them to Megan's mother. They were only too happy to take them and enjoy a night out each week. Megan loved the variety of the constantly changing programme. She saw Gladys Spencer, who later became a television actor and she believes that Vincent Price performed there too.

When a bomb severely damaged the rear of the Opera House in 1940 it never reopened as a theatre again. The following year after repairs had been done, it opened its doors as a cinema. For another twenty years the building continued to deteriorate badly and it became known as a flea-pit, dark and dirty that ended up showing mainly horror films. It was demolished in 1961 and a row of shops, completely out of character with the surrounding buildings, was erected in its place.

Coventry Repertory Company ceased to exist in 1940 when the theatre was damaged. In 1946 the Midland Theatre Company continued the work of the Rep by staging performances of plays in the theatre at the Technical College in the Butts. They went on circuit reaching Coventry every three weeks. The other two weeks they performed at various venues in the Midlands. In the early 1950s a major debate ensued about the amateur versus the professional theatre and the need for a purpose-built Repertory Theatre. The demands put upon the Council for housing, in the post war years, was far greater than the need for a theatre and its building was delayed until the late 1950s when the Belgrade Theatre opened. Amateur groups took on the role of the Rep by giving a varied programme at an affordable price and gave the opportunity for local actors to perform.

Lynn Hockton

Acknowledgements

Many thanks to Kath Deacon, Dorothy Parker, Sheila MacDonald and Megan Saxelby for sharing their memories of the Coventry Repertory Company.
Thank you to Andrew Mealey of The History Centre for permission to reproduce the photograph of the Opera House.

Bibliography

The History Centre for Coventry Repertory Company programmes, access numbers PA2520/1/1-14.
Clippings about the Rep, access numbers PA2313/5/1/1 & PA2509/1

Mary Parkinson (nee Griffin)
A Member of the Harmony Hussars

The founder of the Harmony Hussars, Dorothy Holbrook, was a most accomplished musician. From an early age she had excelled on the pianoforte, being acclaimed as a child protégé in her very early years. Some years later, after two or three successful seasons of concerts in London she returned to her native city of Peterborough, with the novel idea of directing an entirely male band. This being the late 1920s it was indeed a novel idea. This venture was to meet with great success. On marriage Dorothy gave up her professional musical career, but only for a short time. As her husband was connected with voluntary Hospital life she devoted a great deal of her time to promoting charity concerts. It was whilst arranging one of her Saturday accordion broadcasts with the Coventry Hippodrome Orchestra (for she now lived in Coventry) that she had the idea of running a ladies' band. It was to be a ladies accordion orchestra.

The following week an accordion competition was being held at the Hippodrome Theatre and Dorothy went along to listen. She took note of the many lady accordionists and later auditioned all of these girls. As well as this she placed an advertisement for accordion players. From the hundreds of applicants she finally chose sixteen girls to form what became the 'Harmony Hussars'.

It was this advertisement, in 1934, that was seen by a young Mary Griffin. Mary was born in Hean Castle, Wales in 1917. She was the third child in a family of four children, with two older brothers and a younger sister. When Mary was four years old her family came to live in Coventry. Her father was to work at Courtaulds and during this time they lived in the Munition Cottages.

Mary always loved music. Somehow or other her parents managed to buy a piano and pay for lessons so that Mary, and her sister Janey, could learn to play. Their music teacher was Mrs D.B.R. Treen who lived in Station Street. Janey played by ear but Mary took everything in her stride. She was able to play before she was eleven years old and by fourteen years of age she was teaching the piano herself. Her mother always went with her when she took exams, and these she passed with great success.

Mary's formal education should have taken her to Barr's Hill Grammar School, but this was not to be and she passed her senior school years at John Gulson School.

Many things happened to Mary at the tender age of fourteen. First, and sadly, her mother died; secondly, as it was in those days, her school life ended; thirdly, she began teaching the piano. And last, but most certainly not least, her father bought her an accordion. After one week, her father had arranged for her to play it in the local pub, her debut piece being *The Isle of Capri.*

Having left school, Mary now had to look for work. Her first application was to the Co-op, but this unfortunately was unsuccessful, someone else got the job! So, she took her school books and went to Courtaulds where she asked for a position.

She was given employment in the Sorting Room. All the girls were dressed in black and each one had to provide their own apron. Mary took her brother's old woodwork apron to use. In the Sorting Room there were rows and rows of heavy silk skeins. These skeins had to be put on to big black rods and she recalls having to pick up and carry two big rods of silky fibre. The sleeves of her dress were quite voluminous and the black rods soon became entangled inside them. Despite her struggles to release these rods nobody came to help her. A few days later she was summoned to the boss' office and thought she had got the sack, but no, there was a vacancy in the Powers Sammas Room and they were going to transfer her there.

So, in 1934, Mary saw Dorothy Holbrook's advertisement for lady accordion players, auditioned and became one of the sixteen girls to form Dorothy Holbrook's 'Harmony Hussars'. She remembers, following her successful audition, going for tea in Lyons teashop afterwards.

At seventeen years of age Mary was embarking on a musical career. For a short period of time the orchestra was an amateur group, but very rapidly they gained experience, stage presence and showmanship. With such a wealth of talent they soon became a professional act.

A gentleman arranged all the music for the orchestra, and it was he who took the rehearsals. They rehearsed from early morning, learning not only light musical pieces but classical pieces as well. To be a member of the orchestra you had to be able to play two instruments; Mary playing the piano and accordion. Their military uniforms were made by Forsythe, a Coventry tailor. With epaulettes on their jackets and a plume of feathers in their hats. Their boots were real red leather.

Mary with her accordion.

For the next five years Mary toured all over England with the orchestra, travelling from town to town in a big bus. They appeared in many variety shows in big theatres throughout the country – in Bath, the Regal, Southend-on-Sea, the Opera House, Coventry and the Hippodrome, Coventry being some of them. An Advance Publicity Manager always went a week ahead of them to each town.

Summer seasons were part of their show programme, one of which was Scarborough. This season lasted for nine weeks. Ivy Benson's Orchestra was playing there at the same time – on the pier. Dorothy Holbrook's orchestra was in the proper theatre.

It was whilst at Scarborough that they encountered a men's band. Although Mary could play the piano and accordion, because the Harmony Hussars already had a pianist, she had learned the trumpet as her double-up instrument.

A helpful trumpeter from the men's band taught her much about the instrument during their stay here. The higher the note required, the more pressure was needed, but unfortunately for Mary, this would cause her nose to bleed, and they were for ever dashing around for a sponge or a bunch of keys. It was tough going, but Mary persevered.

The orchestra played with many of the famous names of the time; G H Elliot; Ted Ray; Old Mother Riley; Wilson, Kepple and Betty; Robb Wilton,

Barbara Ford (singer) and Max Miller.

Robb Wilton was not one of Mary's favourites, but she found Max Miller to be a nice person; they played quite a lot of shows with him. Mary's father had bought her a full-length fur coat, and as it was always cold in the wings she often wore it. And this was how Max Miller came to borrow her coat and wear it whilst doing his act on stage.

All shows were twice-nightly and during the performance each of the girls took a turn at the front of the stage.

> I know a girl and her name is Mary
> And she used to work at the Co-op Dairy
> Now she dances like a fairy
> She's in the Hussars now.

This was Mary's piece. However, one night Mary arrived at the front of the stage and found to her dismay that she had gone completely blank and could not remember a thing. The orchestra was playing her music and Mary just stood there with a look of desperation on her face, until finally she turned to Dorothy Holbrook and asked 'Who am I?' The orchestra just kept playing until finally sanity returned and Mary carried on with her piece. During all this time the theatre was in complete uproar, for the expressions on Mary's face had sent everybody in the audience into gales of laughter. Next day Dorothy Holbrook sent for her and Mary thought – 'This is it, I've got the sack'. However, Dorothy's reaction was 'It was wonderful, keep it in, keep it in'.

The 1812 Overture is a particularly fine piece if you are a drummer. During one such performance, Rene, on drums, was furiously adding her contribution to the piece and in her enthusiasm let go of one of the drumsticks, which promptly sailed across the stage straight past Mary's head. Quickly recovering her composure Mary had to run after it and retrieve it. Tough and dangerous work!

The orchestra not only did stage shows but performed on radio as well. Radio Luxembourg at 8.15 on a Friday morning, Radio Normandy at 9.15 on a Sunday morning and also on the BBC Radio 2.

Sunday afternoon band concerts were a feature of life in those days and the orchestra played in all the gardens of London. It was whilst in London that Mary had her accordion stolen. She remembers a blob of sealing wax

The Harmony Hussars in Bath, 1939.

at the bottom of the register (It is funny how we remember the small things in life). Fortunately she was insured and was able to get another one.

This was the era of the gramophone and they made many records for Decca. They also played for Pathe Films and Ace Films. Firstly they played for the record and then they had to 'play' again and smile for the film.

The year was now 1939 and Mary was contemplating going abroad as a solo act, but before anything could be arranged war was declared. With the outbreak of hostilities Dorothy Holbrook disbanded the orchestra. Some of the girls went to work with Ivy Benson who was to continue with her band for many years. So Mary came back to Coventry, to live with her father in Fleet Street, above Allwoods, Atkins & Turtons, the grocery shop.

On November 14th 1940 came the big air raid on Coventry. Whilst the Cathedral was being bombed, Mary and her father were standing nearby. The dress shop on the corner had taken a direct hit; they were both sheltering by a wall when they heard the Wardens shouting for them to come away - and as they did so the wall fell down. The planes flying overhead were so low they could see the pilots' faces. There was fire all around, but no water to put out the flames.

On returning home they found that they too had been bombed out. Everything was gone. Like many others, they were moved out of Coventry to a village near Rugby, but soon returned to a house in Green Lane. Mary was about to be married but everything had gone. As the great day dawned Mary went to her wedding in a dress that she had worn for one of her numbers in the show. It had a lovely big skirt held up by a hoop. Her sister Janey was her bridesmaid. She recalls it was quite difficult getting into the car to go to the church.

41

During the service the bride and groom were required to kneel down at the altar. At this point the hoop shot into the air at the back, taking the skirt with it, revealing everything to the congregation behind them. Quite a day to remember.

Mary and her husband, Sam, set up home in Green Lane. Sam being engaged in war work at Armstrong Siddeley. During this time Mary did not forget her music and continued to play in the pubs until her first child, a boy, was born in 1944. He was followed in 1947 by another son and in 1952 by a little girl.

Mary's music was forgotten for a while until the children were old enough to be left with their father and she then went back to playing in the pubs. She believes she has played the piano and accordion in every public house in Coventry.

At various times she has been the resident pianist in the Cox Street Working Men's Club, The General Wolfe Public House, The Wallace public house and the Albany Club.

Mary is one of life's characters with a great sense of humour.

'I have had an exciting life but I won't go into detail.'

June Hill

Acknowledgements

Details taken from an interview between Dorothy Holbrook and Felix Mendelssohn.

I would like to thank Mary for talking to me. It never ceases to amaze me what fascinating lives people have led. Mary is one of life's natural comediennes and her recollections had me in fits of laughter. It was a pleasure and a privilege to talk to her.

The Hippodrome

The first Hippodrome was a corrugated iron and wood construction built in 1884, which was situated in Pool Meadow and at the time was a Music Hall. This was demolished and a new theatre was built in 1906, next to Swanswell Gate. With the need for more seating it was pulled down after being a theatre for about thirty years. The new theatre was opened on 1st November 1937 at a cost of £100,000, adjacent to the old one, which was purchased by Sir Alfred Herbert, the owner of the Alfred Herbert's Machine Tool Company. He had it in mind to use the land to create another section of Lady Herbert's Garden. Many of you will know of this lovely garden in the city centre. In 1955 the name was changed to the Coventry Theatre and in 1979 the Apollo Theatre. Later it became a bingo hall and was demolished in 2002 to make way for Millennium Place.

The Hippodrome (Valentines), 1938

The theatre was built in the Art Deco style; I thought it was a lovely building, but many people thought that it was ugly. The interior was decorated in dusky-pink and seated two thousand people with room for five hundred standing. It was much bigger than the Belgrade Theatre. During the war the exterior was painted grey to disguise the building from enemy aircraft. In 1938 it was made available to the authorities for any purpose, which would serve the war effort. The Regency Restaurant was housed in the theatre and it served good food and was a nice place to eat.

The theatre was owned by Sam Newsome, the son of a Coventry watch manufacturer. He was also the owner of Newsome's Garage in Corporation Street, who were the agents for Jaguar, Rolls Royce, Bentley and Standard Triumph.

Bill Pethers was the Musical Director of the Hippodrome Orchestra. He was appointed in 1936 and stayed at the theatre until 1973. Many of you will remember their theme tune, no prizes for guessing it was 'I want to be happy'.

Many famous stars played at the theatre such as Ken Dodd, Tommy Cooper, George Formby, Cilla Black, Tommy Steele, the Rolling Stones, the Beatles and many more pop stars.

Many of us went to the Sunday Night Band Concerts to listen to the Big Bands and thoroughly enjoyed Count Basie, Ken Mackintosh, Sid Phillips, Eric Delaney, Johnny Dankworth with his vocalist wife, Cleo Laine, Ted Heath and Syd Lawrence re-creating the sound of Glenn Miller. There is nothing like a big band and I am sure if concerts like this were available now the theatre would be full.

During the months of June, July, August and September, it was the film season showing many of the latest films. I went to see *Ryan's Daughter* and *Where Eagles Dare*. My sister-in-law and I went to see *On the Buses*, we laughed so much that when it was finished and we got on the bus to go home, we noticed that our mascara had run down our faces. What a sight we must have looked!

The Hippodrome presented the Rambert Ballet Company and the Ballet Classique de Paris performed the *Nutcracker*. I went to see many ballets there. National Companies staged many operas there and Coventry Amateur Operatic Society also gave many performances. Comedy Shows and the famous Birthday Shows were also staged.

The pantomimes were always good and enjoyed by families. It is probable that many of you readers saw, *Aladdin*, *Babes in the Wood*, *Cinderella*, *Dick Whittington*, *Jack and the Beanstalk*, *Robinson Crusoe* and Priscilla in *Mother Goose* and others (Oh! Yes you did)! And you probably shouted 'He's behind you'. Pantomimes are still very entertaining, whatever your age. Betty Pattison's dancing school provided child dancers who appeared in the pantomimes and many more shows. It took twelve months to manufacture the scenery. The workshops were in the old Plaza Cinema in Spon End and the wardrobe department was in a disused garage in Quinton Road.

Each year the Coventry Amateur Operatic Society performed at the theatre. My uncle, John E. Ashby, always played the comedy role in these productions and I knew Estelle Angel who was a neighbour and she had a beautiful singing voice. As a child I saw many of their productions, as my family all went to the theatre whenever the society was performing. Everyone looked forward to attending the productions and there was always a full house. Their last performance at the Coventry Theatre was in 1980 when they staged *Fiddler on the Roof.*

Coventry Scout *Gang Show* was staged at the theatre and it must have been very rewarding for the people who gave their time to organise the cubs and scouts to be able to put on such a wonderful show, we must remember that these people are all volunteers. I always thought that the cubs were funny, as they looked at each other to see what dance steps they should be doing. Of course some of them used the wrong foot and turned the wrong way. What a thrill for them to be performing at a theatre such as the Hippodrome. *The Gang Show* gives the children discipline and confidence. We must remember that some of these children had not been on a stage before, never mind singing and dancing. Now *the Gang Show* is held at the Belgrade Theatre and as girls are now allowed to be in the Scout movement they are also included in the show.

Coaches used to come from all over the country to see shows at the theatre. It was said to be the finest theatre in the Midlands. Now this great theatre has gone and we have Millennium Place. It certainly does not have the same impact. Perhaps we are all to blame for the declining audiences.

Lynn's Story

Up until the age of eight, in 1954, Lynn lived on Foleshill Road, within easy walking distance of the Hippodrome. Every year, her parents took her and her older sister, to see the pantomime there. They did not have much money, but the event was a real treat to look forward to. They could only afford the cheaper seats in the Upper Circle, or the Gods, as it was generally known. Lynn remembers trudging up many flights of concrete stairs to reach their goal.

As her dad's eyesight was rather poor, he always hired a pair of opera glasses, attached to the back of the seats. It cost sixpence (2.5p) to hire them; putting the coin in the mechanism, which released a flap and the glasses could be removed. The children had no difficulty seeing the stage clearly despite the distance, but it was exciting to try the glasses out every so often. Occasionally they also went to the Birthday Show variety performance, but this was aimed at adults and was less interesting for children. However, it was a treat appreciated by all.

As a teenager Lynn went to see Cliff Richard and the Shadows at the theatre. There was a very different atmosphere to her previous visits as a young child. She was about fourteen at the time and mad about the pop stars of the day. Her current boyfriend purchased the tickets and he must have splashed out, as they were in the Stalls, very close to the stage. She was determined not to scream and shout, like many of the girls in the audience, but she enjoyed it tremendously. There is nothing quite like a live performance, even if your head is ringing the following day.

Lynn's final experience of the Hippodrome came a few days before the closure of the theatre, to turn it into a bingo hall. Mike Harding was performing his one-man show of music and talk. She took her own teenage children for the first and last time and all fully appreciated the entertainment. Lynn was sorry to see the dilapidated state of the building and the interior decorations. It desperately needed attention after years of neglect. It was a sad end to a magnificent live performance venue, for there was nowhere else in Coventry to match it.

We will always remember the Hippodrome.

THE FINALE

Angela Atkin

Acknowledgements
Thank you to Lynn Hockton for her memories of the Hippodrome.
Postcard by Valentines produced by permission of Simanda Press, Berkswell.

Emma Blunn – Wardrobe Mistress to the Stars

Emma Blunn, known as Emmie, was born on 5th December 1918 and at 90 years old she was still receiving Christmas Cards from her great friend and well-known entertainer and female impersonator Danny La Rue until his recent death at the age of 80. This is her story.

In 1961 Emmie was an ordinary housewife, mother to Jean and Mary and wife to Jimmy. She was working as the caretaker at the local Community Centre. Her daughter Jean was married and Emmie felt it was time she had a change. Mr John Evans, the local truancy officer, suggested she should apply for the job of looking after the children at the Coventry Theatre (formerly the Hippodrome) during the pantomime season. A Matron had already been appointed for the current pantomime, *Babes in the Wood* and there were 14 girls in the children's chorus and two principal boys, one being an understudy. As the boys had to have a separate dressing room Emmie was employed to look after them. At the end of the pantomime season, the Wardrobe Mistress, Dawn Thesiger, asked Emmie if she would like a job as a dresser. Emmie was a bit reluctant as she had not done anything like this before, but Dawn assured her that it was quite easy and she would just be responsible for helping the chorus girls change between numbers and to do any minor repairs. Emmie had always been 'handy with a needle' and had made clothes for her daughters and herself so she agreed to give it a try for the princely sum of twelve shillings and sixpence (62.5p). From this decision she began her career as dresser in a small way, which eventually lead to her becoming a much loved wardrobe mistress, dresser to the stars!

The *Spring Show* followed *Babes in the Wood* and at that time all the costumes were kept at Quinton Road in Coventry. After the *Spring Show* had closed Dawn asked Emmie if she would help with the costumes at Quinton Road as the theatre would be showing films and various other productions, such as the Ballet, throughout the summer. Emmie would not be needed until the *Birthday Show* was staged during September. At Quinton Road she was involved mostly with repairs to the costumes. It began as morning work, progressing to afternoons as well and then when the shows started again at the theatre, she would be there at night. So it was a lot of hard work. Most days Emmie left the house at 8am and did not return home at night until the curtain came down and she was rushing for the last bus.

There followed a hectic but exiting few years when Emmie met and was called upon to do repairs for stars such as Arthur Askey, Frankie Vaughan in the *Pied Piper*, Jimmy Tarbuck, Anita Harriss, Sue Nichols and Mr Pastry in *Cinderella* in 1967. In 1970 she met Tommy Cooper who personally thanked her for her hard work – this usually involved laundering shirts, removing stains, pressing trousers and sewing buttons on.

Emmie ironing costumes.

In 1970 Cilla Black had starred in the *Spring Show* at the Coventry Theatre and she was moving on to Blackpool to do the Summer Season. The Wardrobe Mistress, Sue, had been in Blackpool for a season with Engelburt Humperdinck but she wanted a rest, as she would be doing the pantomime, *Humpty Dumpty* with Jimmy Clitheroe. Dawn Thesiger, the Wardrobe Mistress at the Coventry Theatre only wanted to work from Monday to Friday and she asked Emmie if she would be responsible for weekends as there always had to be someone in the theatre in case costumes needed repairing or washing and ironing. Emmie reluctantly agreed to take on this responsibility for Friday and Saturday night and so her career as a Wardrobe Mistress began. She had to go to the theatre in the morning, check for repairs and wash and iron everything that needed to be washed for the whole cast. She also had to take any shoes to the menders at Owen Owen and do any shopping that was required at Sainsburys. It was a busy day especially when there was a matinee as well as an evening show.

In 1968 Roy Castle and Jimmy Clitheroe appeared in the pantomime, but Jimmy was looked after by his mother, although she would often ask Emmie to iron his shirts. These were only boy's shirts as Jimmy's act was based on the fact that he was so small he could portray a little boy. His mother was so annoyed because they were paying £125 a week to stay at the Leofric

Hotel and they could not get an iron! Mrs Clitheroe had quite a reputation herself at the theatre, as she used to cook for Jimmy in the dressing room and it continually smelled of cabbage. For everyone else there was the rule that no food, such as fish and chips, could be taken into the theatre, as the smell would get into the costumes.

In 1969 Mike Yarwood and Cilla Black were appearing at the Coventry Theatre. When the theatre closed after the *Spring Show*, Pauline Grant, the producer and wife of Sam Newsome, one of the owners of the Coventry Theatre, asked Emmie if she would like to go to Blackpool to work for Cilla Black, as she was booked for a summer season there. Emmie agreed and really enjoyed this time and got to know Cilla very well. On one occasion Cilla was on stage having photographs taken for television. She was wearing trousers and a lovely top with diamante shapes attached. Emmie received a message to go on stage and sew on one of the shapes that was sticking out and so did not look right on the photograph. Someone took a photograph and Cilla promised to send a copy to Emmie – she is still waiting!! Emmie liked Cilla and got on very well with her and Bobby, her husband and also Cilla's dog, which she took everywhere with her. While she was at the ABC Theatre in Blackpool Cilla had a large dressing room, which was specially decorated for her with a three-piece suite in floral cretonne. However, her dog disgraced himself by chewing the arm of the settee while she was on the stage and Emmie had to patch and repair it as best she could so that it would not be noticed. On one occasion Cilla badly stained her white costume and Emmie took it back to her flat in Blackpool and soaked it overnight in Ariel. She was really worried because it had never been washed before but when she gave it back to Cilla the next morning she said it looked great, much better than when she had sent it to the dry cleaners.

Some of the other celebrities Emmie worked with were Morecambe and Wise, Harry Secombe, Roy Castle, Frank Ifield, Tommy Steele, Leonard Sachs, Norman Vaughan, Frankie Vaughan, Moira Anderson, Janet Brown (who was married to Peter Butterworth who died while he was performing at the Coventry Theatre), not forgetting Basil Brush and the Wombles! They particularly caused her problems as they kept splitting their furry costumes. Emmie worked with most of the entertainment world at that time, as the Coventry Theatre was host to pantomime and birthday shows for many years. In fact her memories read like a Who's Who of the entertainment business of that decade. These are some of the comments, which show the high regard in which Emmie was held:

1967 To Emmie my fondest love and thanks Jimmy Tarbuck
1969 Lovely working with you Emmy. Luv Cilla
1970 To Emmie. Thanks for all your hard work, best wishes. Tommy Cooper
1970 To Emmie. Thanks for keeping me so nice and clean. Its been smashing working with you. Love Harry Secombe
1971 Lots of love and thanks for keeping me clean! Mike Yarwood
1973 To dear Emmie. Thanks for all your kindness and help love Val Doonican
1974 For my own very special Emmie with my love Leonard Sachs
      To Emmy Thank you for taking care of me love Des O'Connor
      To Emmy with love and thanks from Rolf Harris

Emmie rarely watched a performance from the front of house unless there was a problem with a costume. However, she loved her job and had found that theatre life had got into her blood. She took on all sorts of extra jobs to help people out. In *Oliver*, not only did she look after the children but she also looked after Bill Sykes's dog and took it home each night because no one else wanted to be bothered with it. At that time Emmie was still taking the last bus home each night and because of the dog she had to go upstairs, which was always full of drunken men and the dog barked all the way home. In the morning she always walked to the theatre to avoid having to take the dog upstairs. Another experience Emmie can recall from the show *Oliver* was the pranks of the lad who played the Artful Dodger. He used to wire up the metal chairs to the electric lights and so when anyone sat down they received a slight electric shock.

In 1976 Emmie was interviewed by the Coventry Evening Telegraph (Eve magazine for women). By this time she had been working at the Coventry Theatre for 15 years and said 'It's a smashing atmosphere working in the theatre. Both the stars and the backstage staff are great to work with. People often think the stars are toffee-nosed but they are not. They are all marvellous to work with, but my favourite is Danny La Rue. He's such a perfectionist. Everything has to be just right.'

When Tommy Steele appeared at the Coventry Theatre he had his own personal dresser and everyone else had to call him Mr Steele and any communication had to be through his dresser. Emmie worked with him at the Coventry Theatre and then for 18 weeks in Blackpool, not only keeping his costumes in good condition, but also doing his washing and ironing but in all that time she did not speak to him personally. It was Tommy Steele's birthday while he was in Blackpool and he gave an invitation to all the cast members inviting them to his hotel, the Imperial, after the show and telling them to bring a swimming costume. They all had a good night holding swimming races in the pool but the prizes were Tommy's records! Emmie did not go to the parties until she worked for Danny La Rue.

Wardrobe Mistress to Danny La Rue

Emmie met Danny La Rue for the first time when he played the Coventry Theatre in 1972. This was the first time he had ever appeared in a theatre, previously he had only played clubs and he owned his own club in London. He returned to Coventry in 1976 to play Queen Danniella in the pantomime, which coincided with the premises holding all the costumes in Quinton Road, being closed down, as the lease had expired. Emmie received a letter thanking her for all her hard work,

Emmie and Danny La Rue.

but the costumes and props were being transferred to London. She received £1000 redundancy but was left without a job. Jerry Phillips, the stage manager, contacted Emmie and told her that Danny La Rue would like to offer her the job of his wardrobe lady. His present lady had given in her notice, as she wanted to stay in Coventry with her boyfriend. This offer was both tempting and exciting as Emmie would be looking after costumes and dresses worth thousands of pounds. She asked where Danny would be appearing next after Coventry and was told that he would be appearing in clubs, one night at a time, all over England, Wales and Scotland. Emmie was hesitant about accepting this job but her husband, Jimmy, was unable to work due to his asthma, so she was the only breadwinner.

She was worried about her husband and what would happen if he had an attack while she was away, but Danny said if that happened he would pay her fare to go straight home. Emmie discussed the job with Jimmy and he was keen for her to take it. Emmie knew that he was very proud of her and he would be able to boast that his wife was working for Danny La Rue (a big household name at the time). Luckily Emmie knew one of the boys in the chorus, Roy Ashby, who used to attend Betty Pattison's Dancing Academy, and he gave her a list of places where she could stay while touring. So Emmie, at the age of 58, accepted the job and immediately started travelling to Glasgow, Edinburgh, and many more places.

When Danny appeared in London and the surrounding areas he suggested Emmie should stay in his Mother's flat in Maidavale. His mother had died some years previously but he had kept the flat. While she stayed in Maidavale her friend, Roy Ashby, used to pick her up and take her to the theatre or club, but in other areas of the country 'digs' could be anywhere and she had to find her own way there. There was no set night for appearances, Danny could be in Cardiff on a Wednesday night and Caerphilly on a Friday. He did Summer Shows in Blackpool, for example, for 18 weeks followed by a week in Glasgow, a week in Edinburgh and one-night club appearances. Emmie still had all the washing to do whatever the location and most nights had 42 shirts to wash and iron together with tights and gloves the girls had been wearing. She used to start washing in the dressing room at the first change and when the show finished gather the damp washing in one bag and the 'new' dirty washing in another to be taken back to her room to wash, dry and iron. During this time Emmie was only able to go home for flying visits.

Once Danny was appearing at the Golden Garter Club in Manchester and his pianist, Wayne King, who travelled everywhere with him, had been to a gay club and returned to the venue in a very drunken state, which led to he and Danny having a big row. Rows often happened between them, and Wayne always tried to scratch Danny's face in his anger. This would have been disastrous as Danny's face was his fortune! Richard Mawby, his personal assistant, managed to lock Wayne in the bathroom. Danny came into Emmie's room crying his eyes out and said, 'Auntie Em, can you go down into the club and fetch a bouncer.' Danny always called her Auntie Em because he said he had lost his own mother so she could be his Auntie Em. So Emmie had to go down the stairs into the club where everyone else was in their posh clothes to ask a bouncer to help Danny with Wayne. They then had to alter the show, as there was a big gap where Wayne usually played his piano before Danny appeared on the stage.

Australia and New Zealand

Danny was doing a season at the Palladium and Dawn Thesiger, who had been senior Wardrobe Mistress at the Coventry Theatre before Emmie, was working at the Palladium. She said she would cover for Emmie who was desperate to see her daughter, Mary, who had emigrated to New Zealand three years before. Emmie had not used her redundancy money so she bought two package holidays for herself and Jimmy to go to New Zealand in 1979. While she was there she had a phone call from Danny La Rue. He asked her if she had a passport and she said she did not as she was on Jimmy's passport. Danny said he would send the relevant forms for her to get her own, as he wanted Emmie to go to Australia with him. He had been asked to perform in Australia and he wanted Emmie to be his wardrobe mistress. She discussed it with Jimmy, her husband, and he persuaded her to go. They did not return to Coventry from their visit to their daughter until 27th February and Emmie had only two weeks in London to make adjustments to Danny's costumes, including renewing the fruit on his Carmen Miranda hat, before she flew to Australia on 1st April with the 'British Contingent' as Danny liked to call them. When Danny was invited to work in Australia he was only allowed to take his leading lady, Christine Avery, his leading man, David Ellen, his musical director, Richard Mawby, his wardrobe lady and his personal assistant. Everyone else had to be employed from Australia.

Danny had always refused to fly anywhere so BOAC invited him to have a simulated flight and he came back and said it was just like sitting on a bus with drinks! However, he was a bit nervous when they arrived at Heathrow to find the airport almost empty. They were taken through customs and into a room where they were given champagne. Afterwards they found out that there had been a bomb scare and that is why the airport was empty.

It was Easter soon after they arrived and Emmie was quite upset, missing the family and all the Easter eggs. Danny put his arm round her and gave her a big Easter egg and a necklace with a horseshoe, which he said would bring her some good luck. They spent the next nine weeks in Sydney, then three weeks in Adelaide, nine weeks in Melbourne, one week in Napier, one week in Christchurch before flying to New Zealand to perform in Wellington, and four weeks in Auckland. It was summertime, they were back in Australia and there were no shows, so Danny paid for Emmie to fly to New Zealand to spend Christmas with her daughter.

Emmie was always included in any special outings and on Mothers Day, he said that the British contingent consisting of Danny, Richard Mawby, David Ellen, his leading man and Christina, his leading lady, Jack Hanson, his manager and Emmie would go out for lunch. They went to Circular Quay in Sydney, boarded a boat and sailed across to Manley and went to lunch in a very nice hotel. Danny was larger than life so everywhere he went he made an impression. On the return journey he told the captain he had been in the navy and would steer the boat back into the harbour. He was allowed to but all his friends including Em were ready to jump overboard and swim! Afterwards Danny suggested they go to Cappricios, which was a gay club. Emmie and Christine were going to go back to their hotel but Danny insisted, so they decided to humour him and go. It was not very obvious that it was a gay club – just a plain door and when Danny knocked, a small partition opened and when the doorman saw it was Danny they were let in. They were hustled in, the girls being told to avert their eyes as they descended the stairs. The main area was all set out like a café with a stage at one end and Emmie saw a tremendous professional show and could hardly believe they were all gay men. What an experience! In all of Emmie's experience of gay men in the theatre she found them to be very kind and helpful towards her, much more so than the girls. Most of the boys in the chorus were gay. Some wore a great deal of make-up but Danny would not have anyone upstage him so if they were too obvious they would not be asked to join the next show.

Danny came back to England and Emmie worked for him when he was performing in the pantomime, *Aladdin*, in Bristol in 1983. This was Emmie's last show. After the pantomime Danny was going back to Australia, but Emmie decided that, as she was 61, it was time to retire, as she could not manage the steps in the theatres like she used to, so she retired in 1983.

In 1984, Jack Hanson, Danny La Rue's manager and partner for 32 years, died during their time in New Zealand. He and Danny were at a club, where Danny had been drinking heavily and Jack tried, unsuccessfully, to get him to go home. However, he left Danny and went home by himself. Unfortunately he suffered a heart attack. He was rushed to hospital but died soon afterwards. Danny was devastated and could not continue with the tour.

Although Emmie has had a very hardworking but interesting life, it has been a tough life with long hours needing lots of devotion. However, looking back she would not have changed anything. She has mixed with the rich and famous and dined in some of the finest places, but she is, to this day, still down-to-earth Emmie. Although she is 90 and has lost her husband, Jimmy, in the past year, she is always full of good cheer, and still manages to visit the over-60s club and pop down to their premises in Stoke Green for a drink most weekends. She is still in touch with Roy Ashby. He was a dancer for many years and is now working as a dresser in London. He often comes to Coventry on business and to see his friends and always calls on Emmie to talk over old times. However, her favourite will always remain Danny La Rue. He always kept in touch with his 'Auntie Em,' regularly sending her Christmas cards and birthday cards. Danny died on 31st May 2009 and was buried with his partner, Jack Hanson. Emmie had known his health was failing but it was a shock to learn of his death. It was the end of an era.

Ann Waugh

Acknowledgements

Many thanks to Emmie Blunn for talking to me about her exciting life and for her fantastic memory for detail at the age of 90.
See also our previous publication *Making the Best of Things* where Emmie's wartime experiences are featured.

Ivy Laxon, Just Born to Dance

Ivy Laxon was born in Coventry in 1922, the youngest of five children. Stan was Fourteen, Len twelve, Phyllis ten and Lillian seven. Ivy describes her mother as a lovely lady, but unfortunately her father drank heavily. It was his drinking, which had led to the loss of the jeweller's shop, they owned in Smithford Street, (now the Precinct) before Ivy was born.

When Ivy was a few months old she had to wear leg splints and regularly attended the Crippled Children's clinic. Apparently her two brothers carried her everywhere and taught her to walk, at the age of two, still wearing splints. When she was five the doctor advised her mother to take her to ballet lessons. This had to be the answer to her dreams, for she says she has loved dancing all her life. She began attending dancing classes run by a Miss Booth and became very friendly with a fellow pupil, Carmen Silvera. They took their ballet exams together and danced duets as Mickey and Minnie Mouse. The couple also took speech exams, but once Miss Booth left, Carmen and Ivy went their separate ways, Carmen, of course, went on to become a notable actress. At the age of twelve, having passed all the exams, Ivy became a member of the Association of Operatic Dancing, which is now The Royal Academy of Dancing. Nowadays one has to be eighteen before taking the examination.

Ivy first started teaching dancing in the family's large living room, which had to be cleared. The money brought in paid for her to have lessons with a Madame Lehmiski, in Birmingham. Eventually Stan, who was a painter and decorator, and Len, a carpenter, renovated an old garage to provide a studio. They fitted bars all round for ballet, also large gold mirrors and laid a lovely floor. They called it The Coventry School of Dancing and charged sixpence (2½ pence) a session. Ivy continued teaching there until she was about seventeen. Meanwhile, from the age of twelve she had attended several auditions, for pantomimes, at Coventry's Hippodrome. Eventually ten dancers were chosen so Ivy became a Coventry Babe. The following Christmas she danced in *Aladdin* and also appeared, in later years, in *Cinderella* and *Dick Whittington*. When Ivy left school she began work in the offices of Arch and Company, solicitors, although she still taught dancing in her spare time.

On the night of the 14th November 1940 Ivy went dancing while the rest of the family evacuated to Kenilworth. She was having an enjoyable evening, dancing the jitterbug and other popular dances of the time with a young soldier from Leeds, when the sirens went. They just kept on dancing until the music stopped and they had to leave, so the couple spent the night in a small and crowded brick shelter in the road. When next Ivy met her mother she was very relieved that her daughter had survived.

At the age of seventeen Ivy went to the Empire Theatre in Swansea and danced in the chorus. Once again she experienced an air raid. Walking through the auditorium a bomb dropped and she was covered in dust and debris, but luckily she escaped injury. Needless to say the theatre had to close. Unfortunately, the main stars of the show went home taking all the proceeds from the show with them! Nothing was left to pay the chorus girls so the rest of the cast had a 'whip round' to pay their fares home. After Swansea, Ivy joined a dancing troupe at Brighton Hippodrome, but after a while there the girls were asked to appear topless; Ivy refused, so was sacked. She then obtained a position at Kingston on Thames. Travelling to the town alone and arriving very late she found it difficult to find lodgings. Eventually she found a good place to stay and when her mother visited, the landlady advised her not to let Ivy travel alone because of the danger of doing so. After the shows were finished Ivy boarded a train to return home to Coventry, but had to change at London. As she was crossing London Bridge bombs started dropping. A young man grabbed her and took her down the underground where she spent the night, with crowds of people, singing. On arriving home her mother said Ivy looked like a ghost. She realised afterwards, that if she had been killed no one would have known where she was.

Ivy decided that she had had enough of travelling, so back home again she once more attended an audition at the Hippodrome. There were two troupes there, one was the Zeo, but they would only accept blondes. Ivy was not willing to change the colour of her hair so was put into The Adorables, a troupe of ten dancers. She says she thoroughly enjoyed dancing on the Hippodrome stage.

One night after the show the cast was invited to a party where Ivy met Dick Beesley, the man she was destined to marry. He used to meet her at lunch times and they would go to Greyfriars Green and after the show he would walk her home. After only three months he proposed. Ivy was eighteen; he was twenty-one. The two were very much in love so she accepted, on the condition that she carried on dancing at the theatre. They married when Ivy was nineteen.

Dick had been a fighter pilot in the RAF, but had been medically discharged. He was working as a design draughtsman in an office, but was frustrated that he could no longer fly. He went to see a doctor, who knew nothing of his past medical history, with the result that he was passed fit and he joined a ferry command, the Air Transport Auxiliary (ATA), as an officer. He was stationed at Maidenhead so Ivy stayed in rooms there. After a while, as she became pregnant, Dick persuaded her to stay at his parent's house. A son, Martin, was born in August 1942 so that was the end of Ivy's stage career. When Martin was three months old she moved to Leeds to be near to where Dick was now stationed. They stayed at the Queen's Hotel and were treated like royalty; Dick being a pilot. One night Ivy saw what she thought was a basin and bathed Martin. One of the maids came in and thought it was hilarious, apparently it was a bidet. Ivy had never ever heard of one in those days.

They then moved into some rooms until Dick was posted to another aerodrome. Ivy then came back to Coventry, to stay with her mother and started teaching dancing again at Coventry Street. During her absence her brother, Stan had continued teaching ballroom dancing there. Dick left the ATA and came back to Coventry where they rented a house. He was also a good dancer and he helped Ivy with her teaching.

Life was wonderful especially once the war ended in 1945. At the time the couple lived opposite a chapel that had been bombed; all that was left was a large concrete floor. Dick fitted up an amplifier, out of the bedroom window, so they danced

Ivy with her husband Dick.

the night away, people coming from everywhere. It was wonderful. Martin slept through it all in his pram. Everyone was so happy - Peace at last. Dick and Ivy then opened a fishing tackle shop. The thought of serving maggots to fishermen was revolting, but it paid Ivy to do it.

In 1950 Jayne was born. Dick gave up the shop and got a job as a design draughtsman at Alfred Herbert's. He loved his job and Ivy started teaching dancing, once more, at St Luke's church hall. In 1960 she became pregnant again and had another lovely little girl whom they named Linda. Ivy gave up dancing as she was fully occupied with the family and Dick was happy with his job.

At the age of two Linda used to sit on Dick's legs and he taught her all the nursery rhymes. The family was very contented, until tragedy struck. Dick came back from his allotment and said he had indigestion so Ivy gave him an Alkaseltzer and he started to make funny noises, She thought he'd passed out and asked the neighbour, who was a butcher, if he would ring for the doctor. They came to help her and everyone realised he was dead, but Ivy. The doctor said he had suffered a heart attack. Ivy could not believe it. He was only forty-one and so full of life. She used to say he could make her laugh and also make her cry, but there was never a dull moment. It was terrible having to tell Jayne, and Linda who was only two. Ivy told them he'd gone to the angels. Somehow they got through the funeral, but Ivy was in a daze.

Eventually Ivy realised she had to earn some money to keep the family. There was no help from the Government in those days. She had an interview and worked in an office at Self Changing Gears. It was a pleasant job, but unfortunately she was not earning enough money to keep them comfortably so she sold the house. Women were not allowed a mortgage without a man. Her brother Len stood as surety and Ivy bought a shop, but the people who sold it did not tell her there was a supermarket opening quite near. Ivy used to go to the market at six a.m. for fresh vegetables and worked until eight p.m. to make a living. When she closed the shop Ivy used to go dancing with her sister Lillian whose husband died five months after Dick. Jayne used to look after Linda. When Linda was eight Ivy started The Rainbow School of Dance at Allesley Park Community centre, which she ran for ten years. Throughout her years of teaching Ivy had regularly put on shows, at the

Coventry Technical College, raising money for charity. When at Coventry Street the money was always given to the Crippled Children's Guild.

Ivy met Hilary Warren, also a good dancer and when she was fifty they married. Six years later the couple left Coventry to run a public house in Shrivenham, Wiltshire. However, on reaching their retirement the couple returned to live in Coventry.

Once she became a pensioner, Ivy started a tap dancing class for other pensioners and they called themselves The Happy Tappers with an average age of seventy-five. The troupe wore Pearly Queen outfits, performing at residential homes and Day Care centres for the elderly. When Peugeot Motors opened the Ben Day Care Centre in Stoke, for dependent relatives of their employees, an article appeared in *The Times* dated June 1998 mentioning Ivy's Happy Tappers who visited regularly and how the elderly members thoroughly enjoyed the entertainment they provided. The report stated that 'Ivy's Happy Tappers are still knocking six bells out of the parquet after half an hour'.

Ivy finally gave up dancing at the age of eighty-three.

Jean Appleton

Acknowledgements
Many thanks to Wendy Jeffries for making this memoir, of her aunt, possible and for checking the details.

Bibliography
The Times, Tuesday June 23rd 1998

The Girls' Life Brigade

The Girls' Life Brigade (GLB) was founded in 1902 by the National Sunday School Union. At that time it could only be formed in a church, chapel or mission. However, this rule has now been relaxed. Their Motto is Seek, Serve and Follow Christ. As in most youth organisations there is also a law. 'A Girls' Brigade member will do her best to be loyal to Company and Church, to be honest, truthful, kind and helpful, and to remember The Girls' Brigade Motto'. Members also had to recite the following 'I promise to do my best to keep The Girls' Brigade Law'.

The badge of the GLB has a crest. In the centre is a cross, which is the symbol of Christ and His Church. Below it is a lamp that our light may shine out upon the world. Above is a crown that we may own Christ is our King. Behind all a torch, the flame of Christ's living spirit and our devotion to him.

Barbara was first introduced to The GLB in 1957. She belonged to the Salem Baptist Church in Longford and when a new Minister, the Reverend Ralph Drake arrived both he and his wife, also Barbara, were keen to work with young people and children in the church and district. Mrs Drake had been very much involved with The GLB in her home town of Burnley.

Meetings were arranged and volunteers called for, thus Barbara (Clarke as she then was) became a helper. Shortly afterwards it was suggested that she started to train as an officer. Barbara's mother was very proud, but her father wondered why she was so keen and if it was the uniform which had attracted her! Thus began forty-four years of service.

Having completed the Officer's Papers, Barbara and two others travelled to London to collect their uniforms from the Headquarters of The GLB. Barbara was rather nervous and kept looking at her ticket. The two others teased her, even hiding it for a time, when given the chance. However, all went well and each was fitted out with their uniform. It consisted of a navy-blue suit, white shirts, black tights and for formal occasions, white gloves. For informal events such as camping, a Crimplene dress was supplied. As Barbara worked until six o'clock she often went to work in the dress. She would have a hasty meal while a few girls waited round the table, eager for her to finish, so that they could all go together to the company night.

The company was, and still is divided into sections. Five to eight year olds were known as cadets, later explorers. Then juniors were aged eight to eleven, and seniors eleven to fourteen. All those over this age were Brigaders. They worked on a four square programme – Spirit, Physical, Educational, and Service. Originally known by their full names, in keeping with more modern times they are now known by their initial letters SPES. Badges are worked for in all sections and service awards given for a year's attendance. The girls work for the Queen's Badge, the highest award and they also have the opportunity to take part in the Duke of Edinburgh Award. Eventually Brigade members become Young Leaders and finally Officers. Barbara first became a Lieutenant and twice an acting Captain until she held this position permanently.

In 1965 the GLB amalgamated with The Girls' Brigade of Ireland and The Guildry of Scotland to become known as The Girls' Brigade (GB). The GLB had been divided into Battalions and Divisions round the British Isles, but the GB is now divided into Districts, Divisions and Regions. Overseas work continues.

Barbara wearing a lieutenant's uniform.

It is not all work though. There is time for fun and enjoyment locally, or away on camping expeditions. Barbara's first experience of camping was in the 1950s, in a church hall at Ryde on the Isle of Wight, 'with a lively group of girls and officers'. Their Captain, Mrs Drake, was expecting her third child nevertheless she accompanied them so instructions were given to the group to take care of her!

Special events are well supported by husbands and friends who frequently do much 'behind the scenes' as do the wider family of friends, of the girls and officers, who support GB at special events. Church members too, help financially.

In 1975 Barbara married Fred Dillam, a well known local cricketer. He too, soon became fully involved in the GB helping in many ways, even accompanying Barbara to camps. On returning to the Isle of Wight, in the 70s, the camp was much more sophisticated. Married couples and Officers had bedsteads in their tents; luxury indeed! On marriage, Barbara had gained two stepsons who were, of course, also included in the camping expeditions. They had joined the Boys' Brigade and participated in all the activities and duties such as helping in the cookhouse, carrying out litter patrol and whatever else they were called upon to do. An unusual situation on the camp was that it was held jointly with the Boys' Brigade and also Scouts. Needless to say everyone had great fun.

(Fred recognised an area where he had played cricket some years before. He was fielding close to the wicket keeper and being a joker, when the ball brushed his side he slipped it into his pocket. He then 'helped' the other fielders to look for it until his trick was exposed by the umpire and wicketkeeper who had seen what had happened).

Barbara and Fred lived in an old rectory. A letter of appreciation from a GB member was included in the magazine, The Messenger, after a camp when they stayed at Fred and Barbara's home. Due to previous heavy rain the girls were not allowed to camp outside because of the wet ground, so they slept inside. At night most of the girls had a midnight feast. After breakfast the following day they all set off for a museum, which they thoroughly enjoyed. Returning to the house they played games then had tea. Later they watched foxes eat some food, put out by Fred, before going to bed after yet another midnight feast. On the last day the group enjoyed a barbeque before leaving.

There were many other camps and Barbara says she will never forget their visits to Dyffryn in Wales. Their camp was flooded, but 'the good Christian people' of Dyffryn opened their church hall and cared for everyone. They dried them out and fed them. Many years later while watching the television programme *The Vicar of Dibley*, when the committee were discussing 'The Great Storm' which had occurred years before, Barbara was reminded of the occasion, in Dyffryn, when they too, has experienced a terrific wind. Despite the gallant efforts of the boys, to save a marquee, they were forced to abandon their attempts as the wind was lifting them off their feet! Finally the marquee ripped into two.

Other great times were experienced at the Annual GB Rally held at the Royal Albert Hall. This was a particularly memorable occasion for Barbara. 'The thrill of just being there among thousands of other GB girls, parents and friends was unforgettable. The tremendous sound of the massed bands, from the various companies, contrasted with a quiet Devotional item'. The greatest pleasure though, was when Barbara's district performed *The Snowman*. Every year, before the afternoon performance a picnic was held in St James' Park, come rain or shine.

Barbara still attends the Longford Salem Baptist Church. The aim of the GB was to help girls enrich their lives and must have inspired many to do so, just as it certainly has enriched Barbaras. She has thoroughly enjoyed being a member of such a wide, religious and social organisation.

Jean Appleton

Acknowledgements
Many thanks to Barbara and Fred, for sharing their memories.

Tripping the Light Fantastic
A Personal Reminiscence

No doubt some of you strutted your stuff at some of the dance halls in Coventry. To name just a few, there was the Rialto Casino in Moseley Avenue, the Matrix on Fletchamstead Highway, the Majestic, later to become the Orchid, in Primrose Hill Street, Courtaulds, Lockhurst Lane, the General Electric Company (G.E.C), Stoke, the Drill Hall, Queen Victoria Road and the Locarno (later to become Tiffany's), which is now the Central Library. The Centre Ballroom, in Holyhead Road, was previously the British Thomson Houston (B.T.H.) Social Club, which later became the Berkeley Grill. The Police Ballroom in Little Park Street and the Gaumont in White Friars Street, which also had a café and restaurant. For older readers we must not forget Neale's Ballroom, which was situated on the corner of Broomfield Road and Albany Road. You will no doubt remember the live bands playing at these venues. The musicians dressed in black dinner suits and bow ties and after the interval they wore black trousers along with a cream jacket. How smart they looked, and they were real musicians, not someone stuck behind disco equipment with earphones on, blasting out the music with lights flashing. No alcohol was served and there was rarely any trouble.

We used to dress up to go to the dances. In the late 1950s and early 1960s, it was the fashion to have 'Beehive' hairstyles, back combed and gallons of lacquer used. (Did we all look like Dusty Springfield?). What about those winkle-picker shoes and stiletto heels? I wonder how we ever managed to dance. Oh! Those swollen feet! Other fashion items were the sugar-starched underskirts, the plastic poppet beads and earrings to match, the size of a fifty pence piece. We all thought we looked lovely. The men wore drainpipe trousers, a drape jacket, and a shirt worn with a Slim-Jim tie. I wonder how they danced with those crepe-soled shoes, which we called 'Beetle Crushers'. Their hair had a quiff at the front, just like Cliff Richard or Elvis, long side-burns and the back in a D.A. style, which stood for Ducks A---!! (bottom). Apart from the usual quickstep, foxtrot and waltz, there was also rock and roll and many of us have 'Twisted the Night Away', to the sound of Chubby Checker. No wonder we have wonky knees!

Neale's Ballroom was destroyed by fire just after the Second World War; it was a very popular venue. Jack Owens had been the resident bandleader at one time. Other big bands who played there were those of Harry Roy and Eric Winstone. The staircases and the balcony's balustrade were made of oak, which came from Coombe Abbey. The building had originally been stabling and a carriage house, and later lock-up garages were erected. These all belonged to Mr. Neale, the licensee of the Albany Hotel. Before it became known as Neale's Ballroom, in 1930 the buildings were modified and turned into the Ritz Ballroom, then the Regent Rollerdome, back to the Regent Ballroom and finally Neale's. There were obviously many changes to this building. There was a notice in the *Coventry Evening Telegraph* (C.E.T.), stating that the 1945 Warwickshire Dance Band Championship was to be held there on 7th May, with non-stop dancing to the competing bands and Jack Owens and his full orchestra. Tickets were three shillings and sixpence (17.5p), available from the ballroom or Hanson's Music Shop in Smithford Street. The charge at the door would be four shillings (20p) and Forces three shillings (15p).

Many of us boogied at the Drill Hall in Queen Victoria Road. It was home to the Royal Warwickshire Regiment. During the war it was taken over by the Ministry of Food and used as the food office. Sometime after this it was used at Christmas time by the Post Office for sorting the mail. Around 1936 the top floor was used for the manufacture of woollen garments, such as jumpers. A lot of big bands played there such as Ambrose, Billy Cotton, Eric Winstone, Jack Payne, Ted Heath and the original BBC Dance Orchestra. Dances were held on Friday and Saturday Nights, from 8pm until 2am. One person that I spoke to said that there was never any trouble and you were not frightened of walking home in the dark. When she got home the door was always left unlocked. She also told me that when the girls arrived for the dance, they used to go to the cloakroom and touch up their makeup, and take their handbags and put them on the bandstand and they were still there when it was time to go home. No dancing around your handbag, like these days. Many romances started there and often led to marriage.

The Drill Hall advertised a Special Dance in the C.E.T. stating that on the 20th November 1947, dancing to Johnny Pearman's Band would take place from 8pm until midnight. There was a licensed bar and late buses would be available to take patrons home. This was in aid of the Soldiers' Sailors' and Air Force Families Association. Tickets were three shillings and sixpence (17.5p), obtainable from Hanson's, Payne's in Ford Street, Sadler's in Paynes Lane, the Drill Hall and the Smithfield Hotel, a landmark that has now been demolished. In the 1950s wrestling matches and chrysanthemum shows were held at the Drill Hall. In the 1980s the building was pulled down after standing on that site for one hundred years.

The Rialto Casino was a popular dance hall and was always crowded. One of the bands that played there in the 1940s and 1950s was Arthur Wills and the female vocalist was Jean Hudson. No doubt many of you will remember those days. In the C.E.T dated 7th May 1945 a dance was advertised at the Rialto Casino, for VE-Day. The start time was 9pm until 2am; tickets cost five shillings (25p), and were to be sold at the door only. There were late buses to take people home to different areas of the city. I spent many happy hours there.

The Matrix Ballroom belonged to the Coventry Gauge and Tool Company, and during the daytime it was the works canteen. Arthur Wills' Band played there before moving to the Rialto Casino. When I strutted my stuff, the band was Paul Stanley and the vocalist was Hughie Gallagher, he had a lovely voice. I can remember dancing to the sounds of Ronnie Aldrich and the Squadronaires and to Joe Loss and his Orchestra (there is nothing like this now). Sometimes my friend and I would have a lift with neighbours Ethel and Sid as they both worked at the dance hall. He was a doorman and his wife worked in the ladies cloakroom. We both used to sit in the back of his car and when we were halfway to the Matrix, he would say 'Ethel, I've left my b----ing teeth at home'. Her reply would be 'Have you Sid, well we had better go back and get them'. I would not have minded but this happened every time.

On one occasion, we went with a crowd of boys and girls; it was bonfire night and a gang of youths started throwing fireworks at us. Some of the boys we were with had fireworks and started retaliating, and suddenly the police appeared and took our names and addresses and told us that they would be calling on Sunday to speak to our parents. It really took the polish off our evening. I never said anything when I got home, but all of Sunday I kept waiting for the doorbell to ring. Nobody came thank goodness, as even though I was a teenager I would have had a good slap.

I also boogied at the Centre Ballroom; quite often they held rock and roll sessions all night. When I mentioned it to my mother and father, I was told that I could not go 'because no respectable person would be out all night, if they were they would be up to no good'. So that was the end of that. A while afterwards Mum and Dad went on holiday, so I went with some of my friends from work and had an all night session. It was wonderful (Rebel with a cause)! My father said that I was dance mad, which was true, and it would not get me anywhere. Perhaps, he said this because he could not dance.

Whilst writing this article, I suddenly thought about the Mambo dance, this was very short lived. I was at home practising the steps, going from room to room I did a twirl and suddenly out of the corner of my eye the window cleaner appeared, his mouth fell wide open, nearly falling of his ladder. He possibly thought that I had gone mad. How embarrassing.

The G.E.C. had a beautiful ballroom. In the 1940s dances were held on Monday, Wednesday, Friday and Saturday. At this time the dance band was the Squadronaires, this was the G.E.C.'s own band. The Gaiety Band was resident for many years, followed by Billy Monk's Band, who I am sure you have all heard of. In 1942 this band played at the Stoll Theatre in London. They had won the All Britain Dance Band Contest and Geraldo asked them to play at one of his Sunday afternoon concerts. Didn't they do well! Peter, the husband of my friend Jean played the saxophone and clarinet and his father, Alec Seggie, the violin and saxophone in this band. Previously Alec had played for six years with the Rhythmics Dance Band.

The G.E.C Club was founded in 1925. An article appeared in the C.E.T. in 1992, with the title 'Last Waltz Looms for a Ballroom of Memories'. Bobby and Sid Howe, who were both members of Billy Monk's Band from 1937 until 1957, stated that a lot of people said that if it did close it would be like part of their lives had gone. Unfortunately, it did close.

The Majestic Ballroom was originally the Globe Picture House, during which time it earned the nickname of the 'flea-pit'. The cinema was built in 1914 and was one of four cinemas to be erected in Hillfields during the time of the First World War. It was a success as a cinema for forty years until

1956. The building was then converted into the Majestic Ballroom; it later became the Orchid Ballroom. In the mid 1960s The Kinks appeared there, who had a massive hit with 'You've really got me going'. Later still it became a bingo hall, the Tic Toc Club, the

The Majestic ballroom, now the Kasbah

Colosseum Nightclub in 1995 and at present the Kasbah.

Many people took part in the Godiva Carnival processions, which ended up at the Memorial Park. I have in my possession a programme dated 1936. For Carnival Eve there was dancing at the Drill Hall on the Friday night to the Ritz Band, directed by Len Clarke, admission was one shilling and sixpence (7.5p). Waltzing Competition Finals for the Coventry Hospital Carnival Waltz Challenge Cup were held at the Memorial Park, 8pm until midnight at a cost of sixpence (2.5p). It states that there was dancing for six thousand people. In case of wet weather it was to be held at the Ritz Palais, Albany Road, this also was from 8pm until midnight. The cost of this was one shilling and sixpence (7.5p). I wonder if it did rain?

There is an advertisement in the C.E.T. dated 20th November 1947, stating that the Royal Marines Association would present a Grand Dance at the Civic Restaurant in Albany Road (opened 21st November 1941) on 28th November 1947. Dancing from 8pm until midnight, with refreshments. Cost of tickets two shillings and sixpence (12.5p), obtainable at the door.

My cousin Vic Terry sent me a photograph of a ballroom, the Greyfriars Room, which was above the Geisha Café in Hertford Street. The Geisha Café was a very popular rendezvous and was well known to Coventrians. There might be new cafés and bars now in Coventry but I fail to see that any of them are like the Geisha.

Of course many Working Men's Clubs had a ballroom. Just to mention one, the Barras Green Working Men's Club, which originally began in an old barn, although this really was unsuitable for use as a social club. With the help of a local builder, Mr E.O.C Howells, the Barras Green Working Men's Club was built. In 1913, Mr. Howells addressed a meeting and stated that in a growing and popular community like Stoke, a club was badly needed. A resolution was passed and a new club was built. In 1959 a new Concert Ballroom was added, and it had lovely lighting and a maple dance floor. The Barras was very well known in Coventry. Sadly, the club closed and the building was destroyed by the actions of vandals.

Dances were also held at the Masonic Hall in Little Park Street, dance bands liked to play there, as they were very high-class engagements. I do believe that the dances were by invitation only.

My uncle Bernard Richards played the accordion and saxophone in Tom Pattison's Dance Band. I know that they used to play at St. Margaret's on Ball Hill and many venues outside Coventry. He was a very talented musician and my memories of him as a child are of him playing boogie-woogie on the piano. His full time job was a commercial traveller for E. Laxon and Company, the food wholesalers.

'Strictly Come Dancing' on the television, has attracted a very wide audience and it is lovely to see the waltz, quickstep, foxtrot and Latin dances. It brings back such memories.

'KEEP ON DANCING'

Angela Atkin

Acknowledgements
Thank you to Coventry Central Library – Local Studies for their help
Thanks also to Vic Terry for his assistance.

Bibliography
Newspaper Cuttings for the Coventry Evening Telegraph – 1945, 1947, 1992.

Golden Oldies and 'The Nostalgics'
A tribute to Maureen Spencer

It is more than 40 years since community-minded Maureen and John Spencer began a fund raising marathon that raised tens of thousands of pounds at charity events across the city. Their unbounded energy and enthusiasm captured the imagination of the more senior members of society.

When Maureen and John were awarded 'Citizens of the Month' for their work in the community in 1986 they had already been running Thursday dances in the city centre, a concert party, a weekly musical group – The Nostalgics, a whole series of dance events at city centre

Maureen Spencer

hotels, even some memorable stage shows at the Belgrade Theatre. Perhaps their most significant achievement though was an annual Blitz Ball that had its inauguration in 1980. This event, commemorating the April and November wartime air raids ran for ten years.

Sadly Maureen died four years ago but is survived by her husband John who now lives in sheltered accommodation at Tile Hill.

'Both of us are Coventry kids,' John said. 'I was born in the house next to Bell's Sweet Shop, in Read Street opposite the Singer car factory but the family moved to Randle Street in Coundon when I was just seven. Maureen came from 3 Hampton Road (previously Awson Street) and went to St. Elizabeth's school in the heart of Foleshill. She had two sisters, Ivy and Rita and a brother, Ron. As it happened it was her older sister Ivy that my best mate Harry and I first knew in those days.'

Academically outstanding, Maureen won a scholarship to further her education, but money was tight and a school uniform was beyond family means. Consequently she followed her sister Ivy to work at Alfred Herbert, the machine tool factory not so far from the family home.

The years after the First World War were significant. The War Memorial Park had just opened, commemorating those who had fallen in the Great War. A legacy of hostilities was the large number of factories in Coventry – unprecedented engineering opportunities and a huge pool of skilled workers. Machines for the war effort were being converted to peace-time purposes and consequently the city's place in the Midlands as a premier market town saw increasing prosperity for shops and businesses. The fast growing population meant that its suburbs were mushrooming with amazing speed. It was here that Maureen and John were growing up as teenagers.

Of course there were all the usual childhood games, chalking the pavements for hopscotch, the game of Tipcat Ginger and becoming a dab hand at skipping. But it would be the very latest entertainment that revolutionised people's lives. Picture palaces still showing silent movies were opening around the suburbs and provided a fascinating window on a whole new world.

'The Saturday morning treat was a walk over to the Globe Cinema in Primrose Hill Street for the children's matinee to watch Tarzan, Rin Tin Tin or Harold Lloyd,' recalled John. 'We would buy a gobstopper that changed colour as you sucked it, or a half penn'orth of sherbet with the customary tube of liquorice. We rarely went along without our pockets full of split peas that we'd use in our peashooters to annoy the girls in the interval. But the cinema that meant so much to us was the Rialto in Moseley Avenue that opened in 1927. Not only was it a picture house but became a well-loved dance hall – the Rialto Casino and that's where I learned to dance in the 1930s.'

Maureen and John danced into each other's lives in 1947 – the year of the great blizzard when snowdrifts were several feet deep. It was one of the regular dances held at the Rialto, long before it became a popular bingo hall. Maureen, a talented ballroom dancer, always said that John was very romantic and literally swept her off her feet.

'We both had years of ballroom dancing behind us,' said John, 'especially the difficult years in wartime Coventry and the dances that brightened them.

One Tuesday night I'd been with my mates to The Coundon for a drink before going on to the Rialto for a dance. I'd been standing by the band for a while watching the pretty girls and noticed someone who I had met at a tea dance several weeks before – probably an April Fool's do. That moment would become the most important event in my life.

The girl was Maureen, girl of my dreams. That was the start of our dating, courting and eventually our marriage. The wedding was at St George's Church in Coundon in the April of 1949 and we went to live with my folks in Randle Street before moving to Hampton Road when Maureen's parents and younger sister set sail for a new life in Australia.'

Until that year John had worked in industry as a toolmaker at Singer Motors, later a jig borer at Lea Francis Cars and then at the Alvis on the Leonides aero engines. Now through a chance encounter he became an insurance salesman in Holbrooks. At the same time the couple formed a partnership to buy a newsagents business in Parkgate Road, but it would be the insurance routine that one day would take them back to their first love – ballroom dancing.

'In the early 1970s as an insurance agent, it was a client that took us back into ballroom dancing with a bang,' recalled John. 'We started talking about old Coventry. It was mentioned that they were the first on the dance floor when the Rialto Casino opened in 1937. I was very interested because my ballroom dancing had started there in 1938.

Later in the course of the evening Maureen thought it would be a great idea to bring together old dancing friends at a ballroom event. That's how the first Blitz Ball was born at the Matrix Ballroom. The very next day Maureen wrote a letter to journalist Ernie Newbold at the Coventry Citizen appealing for anyone who used to dance at the Casino, Courtaulds, GEC, Savoy, Neale's Ballroom, St Johns or St Barbara's before the war, to contact her. The response was terrific. The telephone never stopped ringing and letters poured in.

The hall would only take 600 dancers but people queued in the rain at six in the evening, even though the doors didn't open until 7.30. It was a magical night and what was originally intended as a one-off special dance became a twice-yearly event.'

The spin-off was that Maureen and John came to know many of the musicians and their dance bands. This resulted in a live exhibition at the Herbert Art Gallery and Museum with musicians flocking in to play for a series of tea and evening dances. In one of the galleries the museum constructed a replica ballroom of the old days and called it the Rose Room. A photographic display took people back to the dance era from 1920 to 1950 when every major factory had its own ballroom and most churches would turn their hall over to community dances. It culminated in a special event in the Rose Room with a dance band, a Palm Court Orchestra in another gallery and a jazz band in a third. Such was the success of this exhibition of music and dance it led to the formation of the group The Nostalgics.

In George Orwell's year of 1984 John retired from his insurance work. The opportunity for the couple to devote all their energies to music and dance had arrived. The Spencers were aware of the demise of so many ballrooms, dance halls, factory canteens and club dance floors being reduced to disco size, so that ballroom and sequence dancing would soon be a mere memory. Their efforts to champion the world of waltzes, tangos and foxtrots would move up a gear.

The music and dance events staged by Maureen and John went from strength to strength. There was the Monday Golden Oldies Singalong in the Belgrade Theatre's Prompt Corner, a dance at the Tic Toc in Primrose Hill Street on Wednesdays, the Tea Dance at the West Indian Club on Thursdays, open air dances in the city centre, three live shows at the Belgrade Theatre – Blaze Away, Tiggarty Boo and Thanks for the Memory. Also entertainment at Walsgrave Hospital broadcast to six other local hospitals at Christmas.

Their fourth stage show at the Belgrade Theatre was the Nostalgics

Maureen and John Spencer.

74

Concert Party. Where did they find the inspiration and energy?

Maureen was the instigator, John was the innovator. It would be a unique partnership with Maureen keeping a reign on the running costs and profits that went to charities across the city. Among those who benefited were the Walsgrave Kidney Unit, the Disabled Sports Centre at Tile Hill, Myton Hospice, and Maureen's favourites the Macmillan Nurses, the Breast Cancer Campaign and Baby Lifeline.

This unique couple always maintained that music and dancing was one of the cheapest forms of recreation, providing healthy exercise and companionship for thousands of the older generation.

Elizabeth Draper

Acknowledgements
Thank you to John Spencer and Rita Vincent for their help in writing this story.

The Criterion Theatre

In 1955 a group of friends, all members of Warwick Road Church Players, decided to break away and form a new amateur dramatic group. They wanted more freedom to choose the type of play performed and were especially determined to hold to the integrity of the author. The culmination of their action was the setting up of the Criterion Players.

This action came about due to objections raised at the choice of Terence Rattigan's play, *The Deep Blue Sea* for their next production. They were young and ambitious and thought this would be a challenging play by a controversial writer. At the time it was a well-known play and a successful film, starring Kenneth More. However, the authorities at the church did not consider it a suitable choice and tried to persuade the young people not to proceed. Eight leading members decided to break away from the church players to allow them the independence to choose the plays they wished to produce. Despite the pressure put upon them, they stuck together and maintained their stand.

The original core of members consisted of Geoffrey and Elsie Bennett, Denzil and Patricia Pugh, Joan and Leslie Tucker, Geoffrey Eames and Christine Harris. Some had young families and all except those who were young mothers worked during the day. They met to choose a name for their newly formed group and discuss their plans. They pored over one of the national daily papers to review the listing of London theatres, considering that they needed a name that was already associated with the theatre world and would describe their ethics. Scanning down the list they came upon the Criterion, a name they considered embodied all that they believed in. The dictionary definition of the word is, 'A standard by which something can be judged or decided.' Perfect. They toasted their choice in Ribena, as that was all they had at the time.

The church group had always used Sibree Hall to stage their plays and after the breakaway the Criterion Players occasionally used this venue to stage their productions. Mainly, however, the theatre at the Technical College was used. This was where the Coventry Drama Festival was held every year. There were just six weeks to the festival when the Players came into being, so they had to work very hard to have a production ready in time to compete. They gathered people into their orbit, either as helpers or as actors. Christine's sister Beryl and her husband John Smith were roped in to help. John was a builder and his skills were invaluable for constructing scenery. Following a period of intense rehearsals they put on a one-act play called *The Ring Game*. There were quite strict rules to abide by when choosing a play to compete, which could be rather stifling of creativity in many ways, but it was a prestigious local event. Despite having no money they managed to be ready in time.

Geoffrey Bennett, a teacher at Caludon Castle School, was their Director of Production and a driving force in the group. He taught English and words were his business. He was very pleased to have such an enthusiastic group of people under his direction and his ambition drove the company forward. Over the years they regularly competed in the drama festival and one year they won first prize in the competition, with a play called *The Silver Tassie*. It was rather a highbrow piece, which reflected Geoffrey's preference, but Beryl wonders if anyone really understood it.

For rehearsals, the Criterion Players used an attic in Earlsdon Avenue for a year, then other premises loaned to them after that. They had been together for about five years when one member, Reginald Fletcher, suggested that they needed a place of their own to stage their productions. After some discussion they decided to approach the City Architect, Arthur Ling, to see what was available. Three members of the company, Reginald, Christine and either Geoffrey or Denzil went to see him. He really listened to them and understood that they needed a place for a theatre, but did not have much money, only a great deal of enthusiasm and energy. He thought he knew of a building that would be suitable for their needs, a redundant Sunday school in Earlsdon.

John and Beryl Smith lived in Beechwood Avenue at the time and were neighbours of Herbert Holt, the estate agent. He was a member of Earlsdon Methodist Church who owned the building that they were interested in buying. John approached him with enquiries about the premises. Herbert Holt was amazed that they knew it was available, as it was not actually on the market at the time. The members were thrilled with its position and made an offer of £5,000 for the property. They had to set about raising the money by whatever means was available to them. They held garden parties, put on dancing displays and sold paper bricks in front of Lloyds Bank in Earlsdon Street. Beryl was one of those who took part in this enterprise and was shocked to be confronted by a policeman. He told her she was

The Criterion Theatre.

not allowed to accost people and ask for support, she had to wait for them to come to her. It was the only time in her life that she had ever been told off by a policeman and it made her feel like a criminal.

Eventually they had to take out a loan from the bank, or they would probably have lost the opportunity of acquiring the premises. John had to stand guarantor for the loan and his father was so impressed by the young people's enthusiasm, that he put up the deposit. Once they took possession of the property, it had to be converted for use as a theatre. It was the opportunity they needed to reach their full potential, but they required help to get the building ready. They knew lots of people from their connections with the youth club at Warwick Road Church, so invited them to join in and help in whatever way they could. The increase in numbers helped to get the project off the ground.

John's builders' yard was used to make scenery, in fact John was responsible for all the building-work in the early years of the theatre's existence. Everyone had a hand in the work needed to create the space in which to erect the stage. Two schoolrooms were knocked into one, and that provided enough room for the stage. The bricks from the demolished wall had to be cleaned and used again, for they had no money to buy new ones. Beryl remembers being part of the team of women cleaning the mortar from the bricks to make them ready for use. Many of the women had young children, as she did, so they brought them along in prams and carrycots. They were very interested in watching their mothers busy with the bricks, which were used to build the back wall. On one occasion the clean bricks had been stacked in piles, when the weight of them was so great that the floor began to bow. On Saturdays Beryl and Elsie went to Beryl's house to make sandwiches for the workers at the theatre to keep up their energy. They had an electric kettle to keep them supplied with drinks throughout the day.

The Criterion Players became very good at scrounging anything for the theatre. In November 1960, when they took over the building, many of the cinemas in Coventry were closing down. Someone heard that the seats were being thrown out at the Savoy Cinema in Radford Road and they rushed around with one of John's lorries to collect them. When they were unloaded they actually thought the upholstery was black, until they realised that they were just filthy. The women spent hours scrubbing seats and frames to reveal that they were in fact red beneath the grime. An even more unpleasant job was scraping the chewing gum from underneath, but it had to be done. Other seats were purchased from a semi-derelict cinema in Atherstone and they also needed the same treatment to make them usable. As they were unable to afford purpose-made flies for the back of the stage, they bought sheets and dyed them black. Chris remembers helping to hang them high above the stage. They also bought curtains and battens from Peterborough Theatre. All this hard work was occasionally lightened by a funny incident, such as the time when a young man who helped out with the renovations walked across the stage with a monkey on his shoulder. They all remembered that he could be very entertaining.

In those early months they had great support from members of their families. Not just the spouses and sweethearts of members, but parents and relatives, who made a real difference to the success of the venture. Denzil's father helped to establish the bar and Uncle Harold, the relative of a member, not only helped with the building work, but cooked chips and sausage rolls in the bar once the theatre was open. Food and drink were very important, but initially the possibility of selling alcohol on the premises was in jeopardy. As the building was bought from the Methodist church, who were dedicated to abstinence, they were not in favour of its having a bar. Eventually they relented, realising that a place of entertainment would require refreshments. They also stipulated that the depiction of church dignitaries on the front of the building could not be covered up.

Following an intense period of hard work, the theatre was officially opened by its Patron, Mr S.H. Newsome and Miss Pauline Grant on 23rd February 1961. Present on the night were the Lord Mayor and Lady Mayoress of Coventry, Alderman and Mrs Harry Stanley, and the *Midland News* were there to film the event. The press were also invited to the opening in the hope that they would publicise the venue and the work that they were doing. It still looked like a building site at the back and it was necessary to walk across a plank to get to the ladies toilets. However, the stage was ready, the seats were installed and the bar was available. The Players were working until the early hours of the morning to get everything finished in time. One member, who had been working until 3am that day, was playing a soldier in their first production, *An Italian Straw Hat*. He was so tired he kept nodding off in his sentry box. This particular play was chosen because it had a very large cast, which enabled all who had done so much to prepare the theatre, to have a part in the play.

A message from the Director of Productions, Geoffrey Bennett, was printed in the first programme, which gives an inkling of the ambition and endeavour that had brought the group to this point. 'This week sees the realisation of a five year dream; a three year possibility; a two year probability; eighteen months planning and three months hard labour: we now have our own theatre.' The Criterion Players have put on a huge variety of productions over the years, from rather heavy work like *Nil Desperandum* in the early years to lighter works like *Toad of Toad Hall* with a family appeal.

It was a common practice in many small theatres around Warwickshire to give the leading parts in productions to actors who travelled between companies. The loyal members of the company were often not considered for a leading part. The Criterion never followed this policy and auditioned for parts from its own members. This was a fairer system and rewarded those who worked so hard to make the theatre a success. It also prevented any resentment building up within the group, for everyone had an equal opportunity to take a leading part.

Financially the Criterion Players had very little money. If something was needed, it was usually provided by one of the members, knowing that they were unlikely to be reimbursed. Everyone gave their time freely and had a great deal of fun in the process. People did not expect so much in the 1960s and therefore were not disappointed. The first programme lays out the list of charges at the time, which were certainly not excessive. Annual subscriptions for ordinary members was 5s (25p) with 1s (5p) reduction on seats. Junior members and pensioners paid 2s.6d (12.5p) subscription, with a similar reduction on tickets. All seats were 3s.6d (17.5p) for non-members and 2s.6d (12.5p) for members. Block booking of twenty or more seats of non-members received a reduction of 6d (2.5p) on each ticket.

There were a few occasions during performances when things went wrong. One such occasion occurred during the play *When we are Married*, the person playing the part of the photographer could not put the old tripod camera up and it kept collapsing. This was a minor disaster compared to the time when the audience was struck down by a mystery bug. As the actors were going through their paces the audience were leaving in droves, until there were more people on the stage than in the auditorium. It affected the actors too, in the end.

There was no money to buy new costumes for their productions in the early years. It was due to the efforts of two talented women, Janette Glithero and Maureen Copping that the costumes were so professional. They worked wonders to make costumes and adapt them from other productions. The theatre was also able to borrow items from the Shakespeare Theatre in Stratford Upon Avon, not only costumes, but props too. They were very supportive of small companies.

The Criterion Players always tried to be part of the community in Earlsdon from the beginning. When the building was struck by lightning, the community rallied round to support them. There was some debate over whether the building should be demolished and rebuilt or take the opportunity to make alterations and refurbishments. Local residents were invited to a meeting to discuss what would be the best way forward. They were wholeheartedly in favour of retaining the existing building. One woman, who lived to the rear of the theatre, said she loved the lantern tower on the top of the building and would be sorry to see it go. There was great enthusiasm for a continuation of its existence, rather than having a new building, which might not be in keeping with its Victorian surroundings.

The theatre has always been conscious of keeping on good terms with its neighbours. The building is well insulated and they try to keep the noise to a minimum. Earlsdon still retains its village atmosphere, from the time when it was a separate community and quite unique in the city.

The Criterion Players have matured over more than fifty years since their foundation. The theatre is now run on a more professional basis, it has been forced to, as there are so many rules and regulations with which to comply. Health and safety laws alone would prevent many of the activities practiced, while in the process of adapting the building, yet there was barely more than a scratched finger. The whole project would probably never have got off the ground, for it would have been financially impossible. The theatre no longer has the fixed seating so laboriously scrubbed by members, but a more flexible system of individual seats, allowing the stage to come down into the audience. It has always been a private members theatre. This has meant that only members and their families and friends can use it. They have always been proud of the talent they have nurtured in their ranks, allowing some to use it as a stepping stone to greater things. Several moved on to the world of national theatre, Denzil Pugh being an early example.

From an early stage the youth element has been an important part of the theatre. It liaises with the two universities and senior schools within the city, often staging plays from the set books in the national curriculum. Plays aimed at the young bring in their parents and friends. The theatre has never been afraid of putting on controversial works. They never settle for safe plays or pot-boilers and often deal with sensitive issues. In recent years they have put on plays about testicular cancer and a sex change. However, they have retained the integrity that was the original impetus for their existence.

When asked what the theatre has meant to them, Beryl said that attending a performance had the power to transport her to another place for a few hours. Christine said the plays made her think about the issues raised in the play. She also remarked that she heard a speaker at her local U3A group, talking about the word criterion. He was an English Advisor to schools, talking about language. He noted that the word criterion was barely used today and common usage had merged it into the plural version criteria. He said many dictionaries no longer list criterion, only criteria. He pointed out that there were two theatres called Criterion, one in London and one in

Coventry. Christine was thrilled to know that he knew of the little theatre that she had played a part in setting up.

Lynn Hockton

Acknowledgements

Thank you to Beryl and John Smith and Christine Murly (nee Harris) for their vivid memories of the Criterion Theatre. They are still members, but no longer take an active role. They just enjoy attending the performances. Interviewed September 2008.

Bibliography

First night programme for An Italian Straw Hat.
Coventry Evening Telegraph

Bessie Keeble

Bessie was born on 26th July 1923 to Elsie and Frank Keeble, at 256 Cross Road, Foleshill, Coventry. She also had a brother Frank, born in 1928, who later emigrated to Australia, at the age of 21. This was when you could go for £10, and he still lives there.

She attended Broad Street Girls School, Foleshill, where her headmistress was Miss A.J. Wade. Her school report dated 1937 shows that she was of excellent character and above average intelligence. 'A very good scholar, very capable, possessed initiative and was bright in manner and full of energy.' She was a prefect and reportedly carried out her duties efficiently.

She married Ted (Horace Edward Smith) when she was 19 years of age, on 16th July 1942, at St. Lawrence Church, Old Church Road, Bell Green. At that time Ted was a private in the Royal Army Medical Corps. A greetings telegram was sent to them addressed to Mr and Mrs. H.E. Smith, 147 Old Church Road, congratulating them on their marriage, from the boys of Hut No.6. According to various receipts her wedding ring was purchased from Joe Tarsh, the Jeweller, City Arcade, at a cost of five pounds five shillings (£5.25p). The flowers were ordered from Albert Day of 438 Foleshill Road for four pounds and one shilling. Elizabeth the Chef, whose head office was at 23 The Parade, Leamington Spa, catered for the wedding reception, which included twenty-one guests and two children. The charge for this was ten pounds sixteen shillings (£10.80), which covered food, wine and the hire of a wedding cake stand. A little bit different to the cost of weddings these days! The newly-weds spent two nights in bed and breakfast accommodation at the Stratheden Hotel, 5 Chapel Street, Stratford-upon-Avon, for the grand sum of one pound fourteen shillings (£1.70p). They obviously went by train to Leamington Spa, by London Midland and Scottish Railway (LMS) for one shilling and one penny (5p) each, perhaps they had to change trains to go onwards to Stratford. Whilst on honeymoon on 17th July 1942 they went to the 'Picture House' and the price of the tickets was two shillings and sixpence (12.5p) each. After their marriage the couple lived with Bessie's mother in Cross Road. Her father had died when she was a small child.

Ted was stationed during the war in Northern Ireland and Bessie held a travel permit to enable her to visit him, she went in December 1942, January

1943 and quite a few more times that year. The permit was stamped both for the inward and outward journey. The description for her occupation was given as an insulator, this could perhaps have been for the General Electric Company. Ted sailed abroad with the army in 1945.

Bessie worked at Johnson's Wholesalers on Foleshill Road, City Electrical Factors and Ward's Travel Agents in Albany Road, Earlsdon, doing secretarial work. She and Ted had three children, Frances, Denise and Robert and when Frances was a small child, Bessie became a nursery teacher at St. Michael's Nursery in Much Park Street. In the 1950s Bessie and Ted moved to a house at 5 Woodstock Road, Cheylesmore and in 1956 moved to Allesley.

Bessie had always liked singing and her daughter Frances possesses a photograph of her holding a large microphone, not like they use now. At this time she was probably 16 or 17 years of age. There is another photograph of her as the vocalist in the British Thomson Houston band. They had their social club in Holyhead Road and held dances there. It later became the Centre Ballroom.

Frances knows very little about her mother's brief career as a singer in the band as she did not talk about that time very much. Sadly, Bessie died on 12th July 1977 just before her 54th birthday.

Bessie Keeble singing with the band.

Angela Atkin

Acknowledgements

Thank you to Fran for sharing her memories of her mother and supplying information.

Locarno Ballroom

Coventry town centre has seen many changes since its medieval prime. None have been so great though as those of the 1950s and 1960s. As the rubble of war was cleared away a building project began that was to last over two decades. Plans that had already been mapped out before the war were rapidly put into practice. Much of what Hitler's bombs missed, the city planners pulled down, wiping out most of the social and physical history of Coventry. The only evidence we have left to remind us of what an imposing city Coventry once was, are old photographs and postcards.

There were many protests over the grand scheme of a traffic free town centre. History-lovers opposed the plans, as did families who lived within the town centre and would have to be re-housed in one of the city suburbs. To achieve this ambition many old streets and quaint, quirky buildings had to be bulldozed away. Nevertheless the streets and buildings were pulled down and with them went the individuality, historic charm and character of the city centre. Leaving the people who lived and worked within them only memories of their familiar childhood surroundings.

Although Coventry became the height of modern planning and was defined as a city of the future, a flagship for other towns to follow, it was clear towards the late 1950s that the new concrete precincts were uninteresting and soulless. At night, after the shops had shut, the hub of the city was desolate; something needed to be done to bring life and activity back into Coventry city centre during the evening hours. It was intended that the new Locarno Ballroom would solve the problem and its position was selected very carefully. It was built in a prime position in Smithford Way, which ran through the heart of the shopping centre.

It was always intended that the Locarno would be a traditional black suit and tie venue, but even before the plans were on the drawing board a new craze was on the horizon within the music industry. The British older generation of the 1950s, were still very strait-laced, but the young were rebelling and it showed in their choice of clothes and music and the advent of rock and roll. It was the era of the Teddy boy. Their dress code was drainpipe trousers and Edwardian style long drape jackets often with a velvet-trimmed collar, brightly coloured socks and large crepe soled shoes.

Likewise the girls wore a drape jacket, hobble skirt and accessories such as a cameo brooch. The older generation thought the young had gone mad. They frowned upon this wild music and thought it was scandalous how the young loitered around in coffee bars, wasting their money on the jukeboxes, listening to loud music. Girls became unruly and hysterical, screaming over their pop idols. It all caused a lot of trouble within families and parents hoped it would be a one-day wonder. How wrong they were, for in 1958 when the foundation stone was laid for the new Coventry ballroom, rock and roll was in vogue with the young, who had a big influence on the music scene. A new word 'teenager' was invented to describe the youth culture, which developed rapidly during the 1950s. Teenagers of the era had considerable spending power, their labour was in big demand and wages were regular and as high as they had ever been. They were in the unique position of having money in their pockets to spare, in a way that their parents never had.

Clothes and products began to be designed specifically for the teenage market. This was the start of the consumer society and the realisation of a generation gap. Parents could only watch as the young spent their money on fad clothes, music gadgets and vinyl records. The latter were being released in their thousands and unknown artists became pop idols overnight. Rock and roll and all it stood for, still held a stigma, but the teenagers loved it and it created a whole new industry, which is still going strong today.

LOCARNO OPENS WITH A SPARKLE

This was the headline used by the Coventry Evening Telegraph to describe the opening of the new ballroom on 30th August 1960. The new manager, Ronald Bloxham, hosted the celebration ball, which was attended by 900 guests, many of whom were dignitaries from neighbouring cities and towns. Groups of spectators had gathered outside the glass tower housing the staircase, to watch as the guests arrived in their finest evening attire. It must have been a very grand affair. The ballroom itself was lavishly decorated and during a short break in the festivities it was officially declared open by Coventry's Lord Mayor Alderman Harry Stanley.

The management of the Locarno tried to uphold its ideals, smart suits and ties were the set standard for the male population, but it was the 1960s and teenagers rebelled against the stuffy formality of their parents. It was becoming less trendy for lads to wear either a suit or tie, polo necks and casual jackets were the fashion trend of the day. Although many did conform to the set requirements, on occasions boys were turned away and in some cases girls, for being unsuitably dressed. Fashions changed rapidly and became more outrageous for both sexes during the early 1960s. Pleated skirts, full skirts, tight skirts, midi skirts, all went in and out of fashion very quickly, which was alien to the fashion world up until this time. The management eventually had to concede and relax the dress code,

The entrance to the Locarno Ballroom.

when they realised that the teenagers they were turning away, were the very people they needed to make the ballroom a success.

The dress code was only one issue, teenagers liked loud music and wanted to listen and dance to the rock music of Bill Haley, Elvis Presley and all the other pop stars of the day. It took little time for the management to put together a method that suited all types. Some sessions were for under16s and attended by a disc jockey. For the over 18s, modern ballroom dances with the resident band was either on Friday or Saturday night and so on. Once the Locarno caught up with the times many young people deserted their old haunts like the Majestic, in Hillfields, for the delights of the new ballroom right in the centre of the city. It soon became the in place to be seen and the main venue of the midlands to twist and jive the night away.

Elizabeth Draper remembers when she first came to Coventry in 1963;
I was just 21 years old and due to teach at Parkgate Infant School. I had left all that was familiar to me behind, to work in a large city. I was full of expectations, but also daunted at living away from my home and all its comforts for the first time. I had moved from a small town in Kent, which was very quiet, with little to do and never very much happening. Coventry

in comparison seemed to me a very vibrant, exciting city, with lots going on and plenty of things to do and see.

Coventry was one of three places I had been accepted for, Oxford and Warwick being the other two; to my mother's disbelief I chose Coventry. To this day, I really do not know why, except that maybe it was fate, for it was here that I met and married my husband 40 years ago.

Before I came to Coventry I had arranged to share lodgings with a fellow student, who was also coming to work in Coventry. It was not long before we made a few friends and started to go out together, trying different places of entertainment.

I loved dancing especially modern ballroom. In Coventry during the early sixties, the newly opened Locarno Ballroom was the in place to be seen. Contemporary with the period it had a very stylish interior, with modern decoration. The ladies powder room was very plush, with lots of mirrors and nice little touches such as boxes of tissues dotted around and dainty scented soaps, very chic for the time. It was not long before my friends and I made the Locarno our regular Saturday night haunt.

There was always a very good atmosphere and it was wonderful to dance a waltz, cha cha or samba, to a live band. I remember a large glitter ball hung from the ceiling, central to the dance floor. The lights were dimmed as we danced and the ball slowly revolved, sparkling brilliantly, casting its shimmering lights and colours across the dance floor. It was a far cry from the village hall, or youth club dances, that most of the teenagers of this time had been used to.

I cannot ever remember any nasty scenes or feeling uncomfortable, my friends and I usually met inside. One week I was in the dance hall on my own, when a young lad asked me to dance with him. He danced very well and we partnered each other until it was time to leave. After I had collected my coat, he asked if we could meet the following Saturday. Unfortunately, I had to explain to him, that I was going home to see my family in Kent and would not arrive back in Coventry until three weeks later. To my surprise he was on the platform of Coventry station to greet me when I returned. I still do not know how he knew what time I was due to arrive back.

We met regularly at the Locarno on a Saturday night for quite a while, but although we enjoyed each other's company, we were never anything but dancing partners and good friends. I have many fond memories of those Saturday nights, both of the fun my friends and I used to have and of my dancing partners. However, as with all good things they finally came to an end, when my friends and I started to meet our special partners, with whom we would spend the rest of our lives.

Christine Marsh

My friends and I were near to leaving school and starting our first jobs when we began to make Saturday afternoon at the Locarno a regular occurrence. Both Saturday afternoon and Tuesday nights catered for the under-sixteen age group, which were unlicensed sessions. However, this did not bother us, because we could barely afford to buy an orange juice.

The queue to get inside could take half an hour or more, first outside, then inside the glass enclosed, dogleg staircase. We did not mind this, as it all added to the atmosphere. Whilst queuing we often made new friends as we girls would laugh and chat to each other. The boys would joke and fool around, flirting with any girls they fancied. It was nothing to hear wolf whistles as the girls walked across the precinct to join the queue and many a romance must have begun whilst queuing to get inside the Locarno Ballroom.

Once inside we then queued to put our coats into the cloakroom, we were given tickets to reclaim them, but after one of us lost our ticket, we soon learned to memorise the numbers. It was difficult for the poor attendants to try and find a coat by description alone, because there were hundreds of coats all similar to each other. The rule was brought in that if you lost your ticket you would have to wait until the rush was over. This was only fair as many people had buses to catch, so a lost ticket could cause much eye rolling, tuts and resentment.

From the cloakroom we went straight into the luxurious powder room, the red and gold fittings gave it a glow of opulence. There were lots of tinted mirrors for us to use as we backcombed and lacquered our hair into a beehive, which defied gravity. Our makeup was the palest of lipsticks and the darkest of eye liner and mascara. The subdued lighting helped us all look good and after complimenting and assuring each other that our hair and makeup were perfect, we tottered into the dancehall in our high stiletto-heeled winkle pickers, feeling wonderful.

Once in the ballroom it was magical; the dance floor although not as big as those of some earlier ballrooms was still very impressive and had a raised dais at the back on which the guest artist/ resident band performed, or the DJ stood to change records and introduce his selection. The areas around the sides of the dance floor were carpeted and dotted about with lots of tables and chairs. Like most groups we had a special table where we all congregated. Ours was on the left of the dance floor, that way if anyone was late getting in they knew where to find their friends.

We spent the afternoon dancing to the pop music of the sixties. I loved to jive to records such as *Sweet Sixteen*, *Lets Jump the Broomstick* and *Walking Back to Happiness*. The music and dances of the era were very lively and we did not have to diet or go to the gym to keep fit. My friends and I spent hours practicing our jive steps because you had to be in unison with your partner. The disc jockey introduced a new dance every week, with silly titles such as, Mashed Potato, Bony Marony, and The Twang. Others such as the March of the Mods were danced in long straight lines or circles. Girls and boys alike joined in, all dancing together, the chairs at the side of the dance floor would be almost empty. There was someone who demonstrated the steps to us, for the following weeks session. We soon picked up the new footwork and hand movements and had lots of fun during the following week, practicing for the next session, when we would be dancing perfectly.

There were several places to buy alcoholic and non-alcoholic drinks including coffee and tea. It was very trendy to drink frothy coffee in the 1950s and 1960s, a fad introduced from America. Halfway through the session we would club together for a few plates of chips and share them in the upstairs restaurant. We would also have a cool drink or a coffee and sit on the balcony, which overlooked the dance floor. It was fun watching the other dancers and if someone looked good we would copy their steps; it was how we improved our dancing.

Often a guest artist or pop group would perform during a session. These were usually young hopefuls, many of whom stayed unknowns. Some groups such as, the Rolling Stones, Pink Floyd, and The Who, had a large following already, and as we now know, were set to become really big names in the music industry. The balcony was the best place to watch a performance and we always made sure we got a good spot, at the front in the middle.

After we left school, and began earning our own money, my friends and I had great fun on a Saturday morning shopping for new clothes. Once I bought a whole new outfit a black and white striped blouse with a tie at the neck and a calf length mustard Peggy skirt, which had an A-Line cut and thin shoulder straps that buttoned onto the waistband. To complete the look I bought a pair of, black patent shoes and handbag to match, all were the latest fashion trend. I could not wait to wear them and changed into them in the Locarno powder room that same afternoon.

When working we made new friends and our group became bigger and bigger, so we now needed two tables. We also started to go on a Tuesday evening, which was still an under 16s night so the admission price was cheaper. Also my dad went out on a Tuesday night and he did not like me going out dancing to rock music, so as long as I got home before him he knew nothing of it. Tuesday night was when the talent show was held and one of my friends, Jeanette, won ten shillings for miming to a Helen Shapiro song. Helen was our idol for a while; we all copied her hairstyle, a short bouffant, and wore big skirts as she did. Fashions changed very quickly; to keep up we would need a new outfit nearly every week. It was also in the 1960s that the outrageous mini skirt, designed by Mary Quant (who named it after the Mini car), came into fashion and caused a sensation.

I met my husband at the Locarno on boxing night 1963. My friend and I had not intended to go dancing that night, because we were broke, but my brother had brought me a box of chocolates for Christmas and slipped a pound note inside it. When I found the money I treated my friend to a night at the Locarno. Whilst we were jiving I could see these two chaps keep looking at us. They looked very smart, wearing a tie and tailored suits with waistcoats. John had a quiff in his blonde hair, which was trendy then, and lovely blue eyes. My friend and I purposely started to twist and they came and started to dance with us. It was thanks to my brother's surprise Christmas box that I first set eyes on my husband; without it we may never have met.

From then on we would meet inside the dance hall, but it was not long before he started to pick me up from home and we travelled on the bus together into town. One night we were going to the Locarno and I had spent hours getting ready with my music blaring in the bedroom. All of a sudden my mum shouted upstairs to me that John was waiting. I quickly put my shoes on and ran downstairs, it was not until I got off the bus in town that I realised I had put odd shoes on so we had to go all the way back home for me to change them, however, it did not put him off. We have been together ever since that time and we married a few years later. The Locarno must have been one of the main match making places within the Midlands and many couples will have happy memories of when they first saw and flirted with their partner, whilst in the Coventry Locarno Ballroom.

THE END OF THE LOCARNO

Sadly as times changed, the Locarno became outdated. In the 1970s it survived a fire and shortly afterwards it changed hands, was given a new image, and renamed Tiffany's, but it had lost its magic. The new generation wanted a totally different type of entertainment. How ironic it is that now, over 50 years later, plans are once again in progress to bring life back into the city centre during the evening hours. Coventry's centre lost the lived-in and loved factor during the fifties, everything the planners have done since has alienated it even more. How can it be rectified? The Locarno in the 1960s was built and positioned to solve this very same problem. Its success is now being reviewed and given as an example for the new planners to follow today.

In May 1981 Tiffany's closed as its debts mounted. What was built, to be the most entertaining and liveliest dance venue in Coventry became the Central Library, which is one of the most quiet and tranquil of places to be. Although the bars are now bookshelves, people of my generation, whilst visiting the library can still cast their minds back and perceive it as it was when they were young, having the time of their lives dancing the night away at the Locarno ballroom.

Christine Marsh

Locked In

As I woke up with a start,
Blinked a bit, how my eyes did smart.
It's very dark and eerie in here,

No lights, well it's not very clear.
Rooms of shelves with books upon,
I couldn't have read them, not every one.
Then a thought came into my head,
Where am I? I should be in bed.
Am I in here, all alone?
It's late, I know, can I get to a phone
Just then a faint noise, like music, came to my ear,
And figures in evening dress, started to appear.
Shelves pushed back and books all gone,
Folk came to join this merry throng.
Then just as suddenly as they had come,
Music and dancer's went, every one.
Into the walls they seemed to go,
Really I must be dreaming, I don't know.
Just then I noticed someone had put on the light,
I don't want them to see me in this plight.
Now I remember what I'd done,
I came to the library at half past one.
To get a book to read that night,
But why the figures of ghosts, that gave me a fright.
What I had witnessed; was it unique?
This place was a dance hall, very chic.
This is now gone and a library is here,
Gosh, all this has left me feeling a bit queer.
When folks ask me, where have you been?
I'll say into the library, not what I've seen.

Freda Nicholson

Acknowledgement

I would like to thank Elizabeth Draper for her contribution for this article.
Also thank you to Freda Nicholson for permission to reproduce her poem
Locked in.
Thank you to Bill Dunn for permission to use his photograph of
the Locarno.

The Swinging Sixties

Around 1962 a group of ten girls began a friendship that lasted for several years and has continued for a proportion of them until the present day. Their names were Avril, twins Jean and Chris, Glenda, Val, sisters Pauline and Doreen, Theresa, Sandra and another Jean. They had all left school and were working, mainly in offices in Coventry. Quite a few worked at the General Electric Company (GEC), a major employer of women in the city, although Avril worked for the Inland Revenue. They came together when they attended dances at The Walsgrave pub in Ansty Road, near its junction with Dane Road. Most of them lived in the Stoke or Wyken areas of the city and initially tended to stick to venues within that area.

Live music with local musicians was being promoted in pubs in the early 1960s. Previously there had been a bias towards jazz, and it remained popular, but times were changing and young people wanted to listen and dance to popular music such as rock and roll. The Mercers Arms, in Stoke Heath was one of the first pubs to take advantage of this trend and The Walsgrave pub was also in the forefront. It was understandable that the group of friends were drawn to this local venue, where one of the lounges was used for this purpose.

Although some worked at the GEC, they rarely attended the dances held at the factory ballroom. They were too formal for the girls who preferred rock and roll. They did get involved with the dances held at Coombe Abbey for the GEC apprentices. Many of the apprentices were housed there, including a high proportion of foreign students. They were allowed to use the facilities at Coombe and arranged dances in one of the large rooms in the building. As some of the girls knew the apprentices they were invited to join in. This was a great venue as it did not matter if it was noisy, for there were no neighbours to disturb. Despite being out of town, with no late buses, the girls were always able to get lifts from friends with cars. A girl never went alone into someone's car but several could squash in the back for the return journey, before the days of seat belts and restrictions. The situation did not last, however, when a fight at one of the dances brought an end to the events. The apprentices were moved out of Coombe Abbey eventually.

Chesford Grange, near Kenilworth, was another venue at a distance from

Coventry that they frequented. There were no buses for the return journey, but like Coombe Abbey there were always friends and acquaintances willing to give the girls a lift home in groups. They were never stranded and never felt nervous about accepting these lifts from people they knew. The Flying Club in Baginton was another out of town attraction when dances were held there. One of the girls heard about the venue and they went several times, again finding lifts home with willing friends.

Closer to the city centre they attended dances at the Police Ballroom, the Majestic in Hillfields, which became the Orchid and of course the Locarno right in the centre. They often met up in the Market Tavern before going along to the dance hall. This pub was a popular meeting place for young people out for the evening, its many bars and lounges would be heaving, with standing room only when it was busy. The Locarno was so large and luxurious, there was nowhere quite like it. Avril's abiding memory of the opulent Ladies Room was the overpowering smell of hair lacquer. Many of the group of friends met boyfriends, and later husbands, there. Avril and Glenda met their first husbands there. Jean met her husband there, while Chris married a friend of Glenda's husband. It was probably the most significant venue in the city for meeting a partner.

The group tried the Rialto Casino ballroom once, but felt that they were considered outsiders. It tended to be a meeting place for those from Radford and Coundon and the girls felt unwelcome there. Avril believes that places could be cliquey in suburban areas. Perhaps others found the same unfriendly atmosphere in some of the group's favourite haunts in Stoke and Wyken, which was not evident to the locals. Although the Matrix was in Tile Hill they never had the same impression there that they encountered at the Rialto.

In 1964 the group went on holiday to Lloret de Mar in Spain. Spanish resorts were growing in popularity at the time and Val was planning a holiday there with her parents and asked the others if they wanted to come. The whole group agreed to accompany her, which is quite remarkable. Most of them had well paid jobs although many had never been abroad before. No doubt their parents were quite relieved to know that they would be in the company of Val's parents. They travelled by ferry from Dover to Calais, then by train across France and Spain, a gruelling journey of around 36 hours.

They had about ten days of sun, sand and sea before the return journey.

Fashion began to change during the early 1960s. Gone were the gathered skirts and net petticoats of the 1950s and in came the straight skirts, worn with a blouse or jumper. The sheath dress was a straight cut design, still feminine but without the fussy or pretty style that preceded it. Stiletto heels became all the rage and ruined many a floor in the process. Henley College banned them when they damaged the floor of the newly opened college. Mini skirts did not come into fashion until later in the 1960s, with the influence of Mary Quant and other designers. Trousers might be worn for casual wear, but were not seen at dances. Avril remembers having to fight to be allowed to wear trousers at work, as some employers did not allow their female office staff to wear them.

Hairstyles became more elaborate with backcombed, bouffant styles, which required copious amounts of lacquer to keep in place. Not hairspray with a softer touch required for today's styles, but stiff and hard to the touch. Long hair was usually put up in smooth, sleek styles and later came the looped curls on top of the head. Avril always wanted longer hair, like Sandie Shaw, the barefoot singer who won the Eurovision Song Contest with 'Puppet on a String,' but her hair was thick and heavy and never grew long. Later she had her hair cut in a DA when sculptural cuts came in. Most of her friends did their own hair, only going to the hairdresser for a cut or a special occasion. They felt that they had better things to spend their money on.

There was a great deal of freedom allowed to young people by the 1960s for it was a much safer environment than it is today. Parents often imposed a curfew time, depending on where you were going, but you were able walk about at night without fear of attack and common sense dictated that you did not court danger. Dances usually finished by midnight and the last buses went at that time from Broadgate or from outside the venue, such as the Matrix. If you missed it you had to get a lift or walk. Pubs closed at 10.30pm, but Avril does not remember drunkenness being a problem. There were no nightclubs in Coventry in those days and she and her friends were never offered drugs or encountered anyone who took them. Despite the sixties having the reputation of seeing the start of the drug culture, which has such a grip on society today, generally young people were not exposed to them. Avril remarked that she and the others would probably not give their own daughters the same freedom that they were allowed.

The friends met up two or three times a week to dance, go to the cinema or listen to local bands or singers. They also went to the Coventry Theatre to see well-known singers perform, such as the time they went to see Helen Shapiro topping the bill. Second billing went to the Beatles, who filled the slot before the interval, but who far outclassed the star of the show. Although not famous at that point, they were obviously rising stars, and by the end of that tour they had really made it to the top. Their popularity mushroomed after that and they became the premier band in the country. The friends also saw Cliff Richard and many other performers there over the years.

Avril's sister-in-law had a nephew, John Goodison, who changed his name to Johnny B Great when he became leader of a local pop band. Johnny B Great and the Goodmen, played at the Orchid and Avril managed to get tickets to see some of his shows. He went on to have a hit record and later played backing for more famous groups, like the Walker Brothers. Sadly he died, at a relatively early age, in his forties.

Avril's husband, Mick, made the comment that girls had it easy compared to the lads, when they attended dances. It was daunting to have to cross a dance floor and ask a girl for a dance, under the watchful eyes of his friends and hers, only to receive a refusal and have to retrace his steps. Girls expected boys to pay for drinks and he agreed that girls did not earn as much as the lads, and expected this. However, he did resent being exploited when girls ordered the most expensive drink, like brandy and Babycham. 'If a girl asked for lemon and lime you knew she was kosher,' commented Mick. At the end of the night many a young man offered to walk his dancing partner back home. This could mean a walk to Tile Hill in the south-west of the city, then a walk back to his home in Bell Green in the north of the city, as Mick did many times.

By 1965 the cohesion of the group was beginning to break down. As individuals married and had children they lost touch, although smaller elements of the group kept in touch. Avril went to Jean, Glenda and Chris' weddings and she and Chris were bridesmaids to Glenda. Pauline, the other Jean and Sandra were bridesmaids to Val. Once married some moved to different areas and communications were difficult, as few had access to a telephone. Avril, Jean, Chris and Glenda continued going out after they were married, together with their husbands, but this finished once the children came along. Avril learned to drive but very few others did, which made getting about, especially with children, very difficult. Avril kept in touch with the twins and Glenda on and off over the years. Eventually the four friends got in touch and began meeting once a month. These regular meetings have taken

place since 2002, when they talk about old times and keep up to date on current news. In February 2008 Avril wrote to the local newspaper appealing for other members of the old group to contact her. Included with the letter was a

The ten friends at the Police Ballroom.

photograph of the group of ten friends enjoying a night out in 1963 at the Police Ballroom. Since then three more friends have got in touch and they hope to find the others in the future.

Lynn Hockton

Acknowledgements

Thank you to Avril Sheerman for allowing me to interview her and sharing her memories of the 1960s. Also to Mick for his contribution.

Delia Derbyshire
Electric Music Pioneer

Down the years Coventry has always attracted people from near and far with the prospect of jobs. So it was in the 1930s that Edward Derbyshire, with his wife Mary, came here to live and work. They set up home in Cedars Avenue, Coundon, and on the fifth of May 1937, Delia was born. She was to be their only child.

Her early years were spent at Christ the King Junior School, and it was evident at this early age that she was a gifted musician. By eleven Delia had moved on to Barr's Hill Grammar School where she was to spend the next seven years of her life. It was obvious that she continued to enjoy music and participated enthusiastically in the music of the school.

Outside of school, she was also the accompanist for the Coventry Orpheus Choir. She played for them at concerts, in competitions and for their practices which were held in Barr's Hill School's New Hall. At one point they also made a record.

Delia Derbyshire accompanying the Coventry Orpheus Choir

At nineteen she was accepted into Girton College, Cambridge, to study mathematics. However, mathematics and music often go hand in hand, so it was not long before she decided that she would like to be studying music. Wisely, as it was to turn out, the college authorities allowed her to do this and three years later she was awarded a degree in mathematics and music. The year was now 1959, and Delia was fascinated by the scientific and analytical approaches to sound. She applied for a position with Decca Records but was turned down because the company did not employ women in its recording studios.

For a short while she worked for the United Nations in Geneva, but returned to London in 1960 to work for the music publishers Boosey and Hawkes. In late 1960 she took a job with the BBC as a trainee studio manager and so, for her, the door was opened to realise her musical passions.

These were the formative years of the BBC Radiophonic Workshop, and as the Workshop was part of the department she worked in, Delia asked if she could be transferred across. Despite the unusual request, it was granted and Delia became one of those lucky people to find fulfillment and total joy in her working life - for a time anyway. She joined the Workshop, at first, on an attachment, but was to remain there for the next eleven years.

These were the days before synthesisers and electronic music was in its infancy. Delia recorded natural sounds on to tape. Then, painstakingly, cut the tape up into small pieces and then rearranged the pieces to achieve the music she required. Music to suggest dreams, landscapes, under water, future time, space - which, of course, leads us to the Dr. Who Theme. Ron Grainger composed the music but it was Delia who turned it into the tune we know today.

Grainger was so impressed with her piece, he could hardly believe it was his composition, that he wanted her to receive half of the royalties. But the BBC would only credit the 'Radiophonic Workshop' not individuals, so Delia never received the recognition that she deserved.

During her time at the Workshop she worked on many, many radio programmes and then on television. One of her own particular favourites was the piece she composed for a documentary programme on the Tuareg people of the Sahara Desert. Delia was not only involved in music for radio and television. There was music for theatre, concerts and records. She collaborated on the album Electric Storm which is now regarded as a classic of its genre.

As time passed, synthesisers were being used more and more in electronic music, and as a consequence Delia became more and more disappointed in the electronic music they produced. So in 1973 she left the BBC.

After this there followed various jobs - a radio operator, work in a bookshop, work in an art gallery and a museum. Until in the late 1990s her interest in electronic music was again reawakened. She was a pioneer of electronic music who had influenced both famous and unknown musicians and now, again, a younger generation were realising what an enormous contribution she had made to the making of electronic music. It is so sad that her reawakening was to be cut short by her untimely death on the 3rd July, 2001, in Northampton.

Her contribution to electronic music was colossal, so it is satisfying to know that her collection of tapes has now been passed to the University of Manchester's School of Art, Histories and Culture to be preserved and catalogued.

Her music will live on and with time she will, hopefully, get the recognition she so greatly deserves.

June Hill

Acknowledgements

My sincere thanks to Hazel and Angela for their invaluable help.

Sources: The Times Newspaper
           The Guardian Newspaper
           The Coventry Telegraph

Historical information from various Internet sources.

Pauline Sutherland and the Coventry Melody Makers

Pauline was born in Sutton Coldfield and arrived in Coventry at the age of nine months when her father came to work at the GEC in Coventry. Francis Benjamin Stevens and his wife, Elsie Elizabeth, were very musical and always played duets. They were very accomplished and Elizabeth played the piano for singers at the BBC in Birmingham before she came to live in Coventry. Pauline was encouraged to sing while her mother played and when friends and relatives came to visit she always had to sing for them. From the age of five years she had piano lessons, but like most children she did not like practising but with gentle chiding she was encouraged and did learn to play the piano to Grade 6. Pauline was much more interested in learning to dance so Mrs Stevens enrolled her in Betty Pattison's Dancing Academy. She attended classes in ballet and national dancing and also reached Grade 6. She had to stop dancing at this point as she was involved in an accident with a car while cycling to the dancing school and hurt her back and hip. When she recovered she decided she did not want to carry on with examination dancing.

Pauline Sutherland.

Pauline's mother was a member of the Blue Triangle Operatic Society. She was a talented singer and used to take small parts in productions. One show they were rehearsing was called *A Country Girl* and four children were required, so Pauline made her first appearance on stage at the age of nine when she was pushed on, in a wheelbarrow. She was the youngest of the four and had to sing *Lullaby* which she can still remember to this day! She loved being on stage so much, she thought it was so fantastic and could not wait to become a full-time performer. She plagued her mother to let her join the Youth Section but Mrs Stevens said she was far too young. However, her friend, Ann Wood, who was the producer, persuaded her mother to let Pauline join. There followed a very happy time for Pauline, performing in shows for the Blue Triangle Youth Group. These were staged in the YWCA Hall in Queens Road and when a child was required, for example, to be a page in the main production at the College Theatre, Pauline invariably was chosen to take part.

Upon leaving Stoke Park Grammar School she joined Hereford Training College and chose Theatre Studies as her subject. During her time there she learned to do everything concerning the theatre. This included how to direct, how to stage a show, props, lighting and sound as well as performing. In fact she was taught everything concerning the staging of a show and this knowledge has been invaluable for the many shows she has produced throughout her life. When Pauline left college she took a position as a teacher at Manor Park Primary School. The first thing she did was set up a small group of children interested in drama and soon this included the whole of the top year. As Manor Park was a five-form entry school, this meant that there were five classes in the top year with approximately 35 children in each class. Drama classes were optional, but many children were interested and Pauline produced many shows for the school. She worked with another teacher, Donald Dade who was also a pianist, and Sheila Smith, who was the daughter of Kitty Geen (see our book *Redressing the Balance* for more details). Kitty was the musical director of the Central Hall Choir and also the Blue Triangle Operatic Society at that time. Pauline had been a member of both groups before going to college and had re-joined both on returning to Coventry.

In 1959 Pauline met her husband, Alex. She used to go dancing with a group of friends to the Police Ballroom on a Saturday night. At that time there were always huge queues for any dancehall. On one occasion she was late and could not find her friends so she joined the back of the queue. She was certain that her friends must be somewhere at the front of the queue so she asked the man behind her if he would save her place while she looked for them. She searched but could not see her friends so decided to go back to her place, but could not remember what the fellow, who was saving her place, looked like. Fortunately he remembered her and so she regained her place in the queue. Later on in the evening he asked her for a dance and as he proved to be an excellent dancer she was quite taken with him and that was the beginning of a very happy courtship and marriage. Alex's nickname for Pauline was Frou Frou as the first show he saw her in was *The Merry Widow*, with Pauline as a dancer taking the part of Frou Frou. Forever more she was Frou Frou to Alex and all her birthday cards and so forth were sent to Frou Frou! They were married in 1961, but 1965 was a very sad time for them both as Pauline had a stillbirth. However, in 1966 she gave birth to a son, David, but it was not an easy birth resulting in an emergency caesarean. Alex was so upset by the trauma of the births he was reluctant to put Pauline through a repeat performance, though she would have liked a little girl as well as David.

Kitty Geen had formed a small operatic group from the Central Hall Choir to perform shows in the church hall. She asked Pauline if she would help to produce the next show, as the present producer needed some help. The first thing Pauline did was to concentrate on the chorus numbers of that production, which was *Princess Ida*. However, the producer became ill so Pauline had to take over principal work, as well as most of the other things that have to be done when producing a show. This was quite an undertaking for someone who was also teaching full-time. At the same time Pauline was still taking part and performing in shows for the Blue Triangle. Pauline produced six shows for the Central Hall, starting with *Princess Ida* in 1969. The group had to provide all the scenery and costumes themselves. Her friend, Sheila Smith, and other members of the group made the costumes and any proceeds from the sale of tickets were given to the church. One of the actors, Graham Oswin, worked in the toolroom at Motor Panels in Coventry and he managed to persuade his fellow workers to make the swords and rifles for the group. They did a great job in providing these props and even the foreman played his part by turning a blind eye. The shows became very popular and many people wanted to join.

One of the shows performed was *New Moon*. The group had made its own scenery and it had to be lashed. This meant that a rope had to be thrown over the scenery at the top and secured to a spriget and then the rope is brought down at the back, secured to two more sprigets and tied. It is really quite a skill to throw the rope over accurately and tie it securely. Unfortunately the back-stage crew had failed to get the rope over the top spriget and unbeknown to Pauline the crew was holding up the scenery from behind. Suddenly the audience was aware that the scenery was slowly falling towards the centre of the stage. A member of the cast on the stage noticed it and fortunately there was a door in this scenery so he leaned up against the door to support it. Another cast member on stage asked why he was leaning on the door. The audible reply was, 'Well it might fall down.' There was much hilarity from the audience! Also in *New Moon* the pirates board the ship so scenery had to be built to represent a ship. The actors climbed over the side of the ship and had to jump down onto the stage. One actor, Don Grainger, jumped down and took part in the fight, and Pauline was really impressed with his acting as his face was contorted and he was rolling about on the floor. He completed the scene and was taken prisoner. Later she found out that he had broken his ankle, but 'the show must go on' so he did the rest of the performances with his ankle strapped up and on his two crutches!

Another show performed at the Central Hall was *The Desert Song*. As before, all the props had to be made and Graham was playing the Red Shadow. Again he co-opted his friends at Motor Panels and they made his sword and scabbard, in fact they had to make two as one had to be broken in half for the show. In one scene the curtains opened and the leading lady was nowhere to be seen. Pauline eventually found her and she rushed on with heaving bosom. Graham had to pretend to be rough with the lady he had taken prisoner, as she wanted a strong manly type. He was wearing his heavy steel sword; this was before the days of health and safety. However, as he tried to draw his sword it became entangled with his costume. Again there was more hilarity from the audience as he was pulling at his costume shouting, 'prepare yourself, Margot' for it looked as if he was trying to take off his trousers! In *The Desert Song* there should be two male choruses, the Foreign Legion who wear trousers, jackets, hats and shoes and the Riffs who wear djelabas, turbans and sandals. As in most musical groups the men are in the minority, so the men were playing both Legionnaires and Riffs. At the end of the second act the men were worn out by all the quick changes of costume. Almost at the end of the show the Red Shadow is banished from the Riffs, his gang, and he goes to the edge of the desert to say goodbye to all his followers. The idea is that he should come on stage with all the Riffs in attendance. There is a long piece of music with no singing and the Red Shadow talks over the music and says his goodbyes to each man. Unfortunately the men were so tired they had forgotten about this small scene where they did not have to do anything but appear in the correct costume. Graham, the Red Shadow, walked on stage to find just two Riffs had come on stage and he had this very long piece of music to say his farewells. He was very embarrassed trying to think of things to say. He tried to catch the pianist's eye to cut the music but he played every note.

There were many people in the group who were not members of the Methodist Church. There were over 40 members and only some from the original choir. As the operatic group had been formed under the wing of the Methodist Church Choir, and all rehearsals and performances had taken place in the Church Hall, the group were invited to leave, as there were too many people who were not members of the Church.

The Coventry Melody Makers

In 1974 with no rehearsal room, stage or money but a very enthusiastic group of people, the Coventry Melody Makers came into being, the name being suggested by Pauline's mother. At the first meeting of the new group Pauline made it clear that nothing would be attempted until the group had some funds to cover all the expenses and perhaps losses of a show. All the proceeds of the last show at the Central Hall had been given to the Church. So the fundraising began. This included jumble sales, collecting newspapers and giving concerts. The group had a long list of concerts to which they were committed and Pauline had 35 people who were keen and willing to fulfil these concert dates, but nowhere to rehearse. One of Pauline's friends from Grange Farm was a member of the Seventh Day Adventist Church in St Nicholas Street. She said there was a hall at the back of the church, which could be used for rehearsals. So the group had their first meeting there on 19th May 1974 and the Coventry Melody Makers came into being. Of course there was the problem of having no funds whatsoever, so there was no question of preparing for a show. Pauline would not contemplate this until she had enough money to cover every eventuality in case the show made a loss. However, they did have the concerts to honour and although the group had always performed for free she decided that she would now ask for donations. Pauline was surprised by the generosity of the organisations as some gave very good donations. They gave concerts at homes for the elderly, centres for disabled and even hotels where they were asked to entertain at functions.

They entered talent competitions. Though they did not win, they reached the semi-final of one. The group had prepared a number of songs, which fitted perfectly into the twelve minutes allowed. However, on the day of the semi-final the time allowed was cut to ten minutes. As they were such a large group it was impossible to re-arrange it at such short notice. Pauline knew they would be disqualified if they exceeded the allotted time and she told their pianist, Donald Dade, how worried she was but he just said, 'Don't worry about that.' Pauline could not think what on earth he was going to do. She soon found out. The group had never sung so fast in all their lives! In actual fact they were just a fraction over the ten minutes, but this was allowed. Afterwards she said to Donald that she had never sung and danced so fast before. His comment was, 'Yes, it was quite bouncy!' Unfortunately they did not get through but no one was surprised.

Donald became part of the new group and continued with the Coventry Melody Makers until he became ill, so they persuaded a reluctant Les Barnett to become the pianist and he became very supportive of the group and served as pianist for many years. He knew Donald very well as they were both teachers. They used to play duets together and were known locally as Ravitz and Landauer, a very popular act who regularly appeared on the television.

When the Coventry Melody Makers had sufficient money for Pauline to think about staging a show, she wanted to choose one where they could make their own scenery and costumes. So the first show, *Viva Mexico*, was performed at the Sibree Hall in September 1975. The founder members of the Coventry Melody Makers involved with the first show were Graham Oswin, Jim Woodhouse, Bill Walton, Tim Eden, Dwynwyn Langford, Susan Woodhead, Sheila and Reg Payne, Barbara Howard, Judith Hancox, Ralph Mounter, Joe Waugh, Ann Newell, Harold Wood, Lucy Costello, Morva and Doreen Jones, John and Margaret Davis, Kay, Philip and Paul Hallmark, Philip Atkinson, Eileen Kenny, Carol Lewis, Peter Morley, Alexandra Holliday and Dick and Pat Kirkland. Sadly a number of these people have passed on or moved away. However, there are still four from the first show, *Viva Mexico*, staged 35 years ago, who are still present-day members – Pauline, Graham Oswin, Jim Woodhouse and Lucy Costello.

It was great fun staging *Viva Mexico* but also a lot of hard work. In the show there is a song called, 'Give her a Rose for her Hair' and it was decided to present every lady in the audience with a fresh rose as they came in. These were scrounged, begged or skilfully removed from neighbours' gardens. Over 150 were prepared and presented at the last night's performance. The show was a resounding success and the Melody Makers, to their delight, made quite a lot of money from this first show. Pauline was so heartened by this success that it was decided to stage the next show at the College Theatre.

During a social outing on the Pearl Hyde narrow boat, the group met Ken Squires, a local businessman. He was very interested in what they were doing and wanted to be involved. He was asked to be President of the society and he generously agreed to pay for the cost of hiring the College Theatre for the next group production, *White Horse Inn*. Ken continued to support the Coventry Melody Makers for many years until his death. The role of President has now been accepted by his son, Doug Squires, who remains very supportive to this day. *White Horse Inn* was also a great success and because of this the Melody Makers decided to support local charities and donate part of the proceeds. Over the years, they have donated in excess of £12,000 to local charities.

The following shows were all staged at the College Theatre:

1975	*White Horse Inn*	1988	*Mr Cinders*
1976	*Finian's Rainbow*	1989	*The Forties and All That*
1978	*Love From Judy*	1989	*Seven Brides For Seven Brothers*
1979	*The Quaker Girl*	1990	*East is East and West is West*
1980	*Rio Rita*		*The Student Prince*
1981	*Belle of New York*	1991	*Jan: Crufts Centenary Pageant*
1982	*Them Thar Hills*		*March: Music Hall*
	Me and My Girl		*July: A Musical Celebration*
1983	*Gypsy Baron*		*Sept: Girl Crazy*
1984	*Bless the Bride*	1992	*Melody Makers' Minstrel Show*
1985	*Zip Goes a Million*	1993	*Another Minstrel Show*
1986	*La Belle Helene*	1995	*Salad Days*
1987	*Viva Mexico!*	1996	*Where's Charley*
1988	*A Musical Celebration*		

Performances at the College Theatre were preceded by many hours of hard work, particularly for Pauline, as Director. She had to stage the production, make sure the lighting was organised, spotlights were in the correct places, as well as to design and produce the programme. Many other people were responsible for wardrobe, stage management, make-up, photography, props, publicity and box office and most of these people were also part of the cast. Shows were performed from Wednesday to Saturday with a matinee in the afternoon. Tuesday was first night at the College Theatre and used to be donations only. This performance was mainly for pensioner and disabled groups, to whom the Coventry Melody Makers had given concerts. Unfortunately some organisations abused this privilege and extended invitations to relatives and friends. This resulted in a lower attendance for the ticketed shows and consequently less revenue. Therefore a small charge for Tuesday evening had to be made.

It was a long but enjoyable week of hard work. Everyone had to arrive early at their allotted dressing rooms in time to get their make-up on. It was a hive of activity behind the stage. Nerves were taut as the time came for members of the cast to enter the stage at the right time and remember words, songs, moves and where they were supposed to be on stage. It was particularly unnerving if the wrong cue was given or a fellow actor forgot the words, but everything turned out well in the end. The cast became very good at ad-libbing. Saturday night was always the best night. Everyone was excited, presents were exchanged between the cast and there was a sense of relief that the hard work was over, coupled with sadness that the show had come to an end. However, there was always the after-show party to look forward to.

Pauline turned a blind eye to 'last night tricks' although they were discouraged as they could cause actors

The Melody Makers in Bless the Bride, 1984.

110

to forget their lines. In *Finian's Rainbow* there were rubber snakes, spiders and other insects in the sack of corn and in *Love From Judy* the young ladies were on stage and were offered a biscuit from a biscuit tin. There was one biscuit for each girl and on the last night a picture of a naked man had been pasted to the bottom of the tin! There were a few giggles and ad-libs from the girls asking for an extra biscuit. In *Seven Brides For Seven Brothers*, when the brides and brothers looked into the cot, the baby had a big black moustache! This show was also memorable as it had the largest audience the group had ever had, due to the fact that the Coventry Melody Makers were the first group to perform this musical in Coventry. Concerts were also very demanding. They were invited to perform at the NEC for the Crufts Centenary Pageant and also at the Hotel Metropole with the Ken Mackintosh band and the Joe Loss Band. On the 50th anniversary of World War Two the group sang on the balcony at the Hotel Leofric as a warm up to Vera Lynn, then had to dash to Christ the King for a Blitz Ball, and then back to the Leofric for another spot at their Blitz Ball.

In the early days there were many family groups taking part in the shows. Husbands and wives and their children grew up enjoying the companionship of other families, not only on the stage, but on outings to the seaside, pony trekking, trips abroad and many, many parties. One couple, Wendy and Peter Gibbons met through their involvement with the Coventry Melody Makers. They married and called their little girl, Melody. The group lost a lot of young members in 1996 as university and careers beckoned so it was decided to stage one big concert each year at a smaller venue. Although they were a smaller group they still worked hard to stage an annual production. Many of these were staged at Allesley Village Hall.

Coventry Melody Makers – 35 Years

Coventry Melody Makers are still performing and this year is their 35th Anniversary. Concerts are still given to any group that makes a request and the number of concerts is usually 25-30 each year. Many of the concerts are given in the morning or afternoon so only those members who are retired can attend, although in the evening they are attended by the majority of the group. Pauline plans the concert around those attending so it consists of chorus numbers and solos, always with a touch of humour in the form of jokes and monologues. Graham Oswin and Jim Woodhouse, two of the original members, usually act as comperes, and Shirley Denyer, the pianist for several years, is always there to keep everyone on the right note. No charge is made but donations are acceptable as this enables the group to stage a show each year. Coventry Melody Makers, unlike other companies who perform shows, have always been run on an entirely voluntary basis. No one receives any reward apart from the satisfaction and enjoyment of performing and giving pleasure to other people.

Pauline still puts together and takes part in the annual show. Members are encouraged to select songs and sketches they would like to do and Pauline includes many chorus numbers and in the past has written a storyline to fit around the songs. However, in 2008 Phil McGuinness, a member since 1986, wrote *Musical Mysteries* and he is working on his next show, *Mum's Army*, for 2010. In 2006 the Coventry Melody Makers moved to the Hearsall Baptist Church Hall and that is where their annual show has been staged for the past four years.

The Coventry Melody Makers meet every Tuesday evening at Allesley Church Hall to practise their singing and it is always an enjoyable evening. The social life of the group has to be less demanding these days as the group grows older but there is always a Christmas party and a strawberry tea at Pauline's house in the summer.

Coventry Melody Makers have brought a great deal of pleasure and enjoyment to many groups and audiences over the past 35 years. The organisation of the group has been a large part of Pauline Sutherland's life and she is still as enthusiastic to this day.

Ann Waugh

Acknowledgements

Many thanks to Pauline for her time given to my many questions and to Graham Oswin, Jim Woodhouse and Lucy Costello for their reminiscences.

Thank you to Ron Shandley for allowing us to reproduce his photograph of the Coventry Melody Makers in costume for the production of *Bless the Bride* in October 1984.

Just Bowling Along

The game of bowls, as played today, became popular in the thirteenth century, but in the early fourteenth century Edward III banned the game, along with other sports. He was concerned that archery skills were being neglected and they were necessary to fight the many wars in Europe at the time. However, the ban did not last long. It was not until 1900 that women took up the sport. The English Bowling Association was formed in 1903. It was not until 1931 that The English Women's Bowling Association was formed. Eventually in January 2008 the two associations merged to become Bowls England in keeping with modern parlance.

' . . . . it's the best thing that I have ever done in my life.' Thus says Anita Smith on her decision to start playing bowls.

Anita worked as a telephonist for the Post Office. Having worked all the week she found herself spending the weekends gardening, clipping hedges and mowing the lawn. Her husband meanwhile, was out playing golf. She complained to a friend how frustrated she felt and her friend suggested that Anita should try playing bowls with her at the Coventry Gauge and Tool Sports Ground. This later became the Matrix Bowling Club and is now known as the Highway Sports Club. She thought about it and told her husband that she was going to have a look at the club. This was the start of 'thirty-four years of wonderful sport and friendship'.

It was in 1975 that Anita joined the club, to play flat green bowls. Flat green bowls is played straight up and down a green. In 1981 she became Captain of the Ladies Section. She held this position several times thereafter, a position she greatly enjoyed. In 1986 she became Lady Chair, a post she held for ten years. During those years Anita says that she probably did as much as anyone, to put ladies bowls on the map, as far as Highway was concerned. One change she made at her club was to encourage the men to ask their wives to organise club teas on match days. Hitherto the lady bowlers had done this, which meant not being available to play, themselves, leaving the team short.

The men's bowls teams held annual galas, so with help from Brian Simmons, secretary of the men's section, Anita set about organising a

Ladies Gala, which was to be the first such event to be held in Warwickshire. Nineteen teams entered which was not a sufficient number. As her club also had a ladies crown green bowling section Anita approached them to ask whether any of their members would be interested in making up the twentieth team. Playing on a crown green surface was different, from flat green bowling, as the name implies. Crown green bowls is played on a square lawn which rises slightly in the centre and the players bowl in any direction. Nevertheless, any bowler who played indoor bowls was used to a flat surface and Anita obtained some volunteers. Crown green bowlers did not wear uniforms, so Anita explained the dress code stating that white clothing was to be worn.

It was hard work arranging the event, which involved organising the food, the teams, and buying the prizes. It had been decided not to award money, but to buy cut glassware rather than inscribed trophies. Anita knew from experience that such items were never used. The day duly arrived and the ladies turned up suitably attired in white, including the crown green bowlers, but horror of horrors one of their members was wearing a mini-skirt! Some county bowlers had agreed to play and one can only imagine them wondering what they had let themselves in for. Nevertheless, all went well and after the matches the prizes were awarded, a raffle was held and to round things off a lovely meal was served. A fitting end to what had been a most successful day. That was the beginning of Ladies Galas in Warwickshire. Eventually other clubs followed suit, but it was a first for Anita and the ladies section of the club.

In 1990 the club had a very good bowling coach, Peter Eykyn, and under his instruction Anita became an instructor and eventually a coach. It was Peter who really inspired her. Anita says 'I've always felt interested in putting something back into the game, which has given me so much pleasure'. She is still coaching which she greatly enjoys, especially if she can get young people involved. This is one of her main concerns. There is little interest shown, by many of the older generation, to encourage young people to play. She thinks that this is a very selfish attitude. While there are a few youngsters involved, there are not nearly enough. Anita has suggested, to bowlers at the Coventry indoor rink, that they approach the two sports colleges in the area to offer coaching to the students. She thinks that young people would try the sport and while they might not continue with it then, in later years they could return to the game. Unfortunately, some of the senior bowlers do not encourage youngsters. One seventy-five year old asked why there was a need, perhaps fearing she would lose her place in the team. She is still bowling for the county, which proves that if you are good enough you will still be picked, whatever your age. Even getting the forty to fifty year olds into the sport is proving difficult. She thinks it very sad and envisages the folding of some local clubs if more is not done to enrol new members.

Later, in 1994, Anita passed the Marker's exam enabling her to become a marker for England matches. A Marker is responsible for the rules being adhered to. They answer questions and measure any disputed shots. This exam has to be retaken every five years, but when the time came for her to re-sit, her husband had become very ill and subsequently died. Understandably, for a while, she lost interest in studying to take the exams again. Therefore, officially Anita is no longer qualified to mark or umpire. Yet, having said that, she now does more marking and more umpiring,

Anita wearing Marker's Uniform.

than she has ever done, due to a shortage of others qualified to officiate. She is now more involved in county marking and umpiring, including the prestigious annual county competitions held at Leamington Spa. Ten years ago no one without a certificate of qualification would have been allowed to officiate. Though Anita is not technically qualified, she certainly is well experienced. Already she has been sent a list of matches for the forthcoming season, requesting her to officiate,

One thing Anita never did, was apply to play for the county. Although she was a good enough bowler to have done so, it never appealed to her.

She says she thought it was very elitist at the time, although this is not the case now. County games were always played on a Wednesday and as Anita worked it would have been difficult, and also expensive, to buy the uniform to play only occasionally. She does though, have the satisfaction of knowing that club opponents respected her and saw playing against her a real challenge.

Much has changed since Anita began playing bowls. Bowlers never played without wearing a hat and a uniform of cream or white. Coloured clothing was not allowed, except for club colours on the women's hat bands. Now rules have been relaxed. Coloured tops are acceptable and trousers may be worn. Hats are not compulsory, although there is an approved range of headwear available. The etiquette has more or less disappeared which is to be regretted, for etiquette was very much part of the game in Anita's early days. When she was captain she always went into the car park and greeted visiting teams as they arrived. 'I always made sure that every member of the visiting team was escorted to tea and back onto the green when play resumed. At the end of the game I always went to the car park to say goodbye. It was not only me who did that it was the standard of etiquette in those early days. That has gone and I think it is to the detriment of the sport'. Anita considers the only downside, in the sport, to be what is said or done on the greens these days, but she realises that one person cannot change things.

There have been several memorable events during Anita's bowling career to date. In 1980 the Ladies World Bowls was to be held in Toronto, Canada. Mrs Rollason, Vice-President of England Women's Bowls Association and a member of Coventry Three Spires Bowling Club, asked Anita if she would like to join her and the Warwickshire Ladies on the trip. Anita's husband encouraged her to go. However, considering the cost and the fact that they had two teenage children, she declined, even though she had relatives in Toronto. Ruefully, she says 'perhaps that's my biggest regret. I should have gone. I had the opportunity and I didn't take it.'

Another occasion concerns the day that Coventry City played for, and won, the F.A. Cup in 1987. The ladies were playing at home against Bournville Ladies. From the row of houses, at one side of the ground, could be heard the televisions while the A45 on the other side was absolutely silent. Once the final whistle went, within seconds it was alive with traffic. 'We did stop the game for five minutes, because even my ladies were excited, though I don't think the Bournville team was impressed.'

Anita considers herself to have been very lucky in the things she has done. Perhaps of all the special occasions the highlight came in 1996. The World Bowls competition was held at Leamington Spa and she was asked to be a reserve for Warwickshire, who were going to play the Rest of the World, in a pre-match tournament warm-up. Ten minutes before the game started her name was called over the Tannoy system asking her to report to the office. There they asked her if she would play for Israel as one of their players was injured and they had no reserve. She agreed to do so, but felt very nervous. They were on an end rink and were playing against Warwickshire. Anita asked the Israeli skip which position she wished her to play, thinking she would be playing two, which was always considered the weakest spot in the team, although Anita is not of that opinion. Much to her surprise she was asked to play number three. On the first end, when it was her turn to bowl, she asked the skip what she wanted her to do. The skip said she wanted Anita to place her bowl to finish eight to ten inches behind the jack. Anita did just that. From then on she felt very confident that she would not let the Israeli team down. Her rink went on to beat the Warwickshire rink 28-4. Afterwards Anita was included in the invitation to a civic reception in the marquee where she sat with the Israeli team. It turned out to have been a wonderful day.

Despite being fully committed to her own club, Anita and several others made time to help   disabled bowlers, at the West Midlands Sports Centre, once a week. She was present at the Official Opening of the centre, by His Royal Highness, The Duke of Kent.

In 2006 Anita attended a coaching course for four days in Somerset, run by David Bryant, a legend in the bowling world. Anita applied sending her resume as requested and to her delight was accepted. She stayed at her daughter's home in Dorset and drove over to the course venue daily, a journey of thirty or so miles. Anita said that meeting the bowler was such a wonderful experience. 'David Bryant is the same face to face as he is on the television, a complete and utter gentleman. I learned more in those few days than I had learned in the previous thirty years. It was the most fantastic four days I have ever had. I learned so much.' Anita considers him to be the best ambassador any sport could have. She thinks bowling is lucky to have him. He is quite her hero.

In the early 1980s Anita's husband had joined the club and both eventually retired from work. The men's and ladies teams at the club usually played on different days, or at varying times, so the couple hardly saw each other. In 1997 they decided to move to Corley Bowls Club, where mixed matches were played, which proved to have been a good move. Here too, Anita has been Ladies Captain.

'I would like to think that people coming into the game now would have thirty-four years like I have had, of absolutely wonderful sport and friendship. I walked into an indoor gala recently and was greeted by bowlers I have frequently played with, or against, over the years. There's this lovely camaraderie. I only hope I can carry on for a few more years'.

Jean Appleton

Anita was interviewed in February 2009.

The Bard of Sherbourne

Children have always loved dressing up and most enjoy singing and dancing. Many schools put on theatrical productions and musical events, especially in the past when the rigors of the curriculum were not so onerous. Imagine what it was like for a school catering for children with physical and mental disabilities. One such school in Coventry was Sherbourne Fields in Coundon that staged many productions in the 1970s, in which all the children were involved.

They were instigated by Ann Harris, a teacher at the school, with the support of John Pollard, a well-known musician in the city and fellow teacher at the school. Another member of staff, Shirley Wensley, who had been a dancer, was roped in to organize the choreography. Ann spoke to the Head, Gerry Murphy, about putting on a twenty-minute drama about a famine in India and his enthusiastic support lent impetus to the idea. This production took place in about 1972 and proved a great success. It encouraged the team to try a more ambitious performance of *Joseph and his Technicolour Dreamcoat*, which was extended by narration and movement. Following this a drama was staged about Noah and the floating zoo.

Lesley Grove, who taught at the school, took her mother Dorothy Parker, along to see *Joseph and his Technicolour Dreamcoat* and she thoroughly enjoyed it. She was very impressed by the way they had involved all the children no matter to what extent they were disabled. In about 1974 Dorothy was asked to write a pantomime lasting about an

Dorothy Parker

hour for the children, bearing in mind that every child had to be included in some way. Dorothy had always had an interest in music and drama, although up to that point her only experience of writing had been a short dramatic piece in rhyming couplets for the Women's Institute drama group and odds and ends for the church. It was quite a challenge, but she agreed to have a go.

The first pantomime she wrote was based on *Snow White and the Seven Dwarfs*. She had to think about the age range of the children, from three-year olds to teenagers, including wheelchair users. Another factor in her calculations was the problem of children being sent for treatment or consultations without much notice. It was no good having a title with a specific number, like seven dwarfs, as there might only be six on the day of the performance. She solved the problem by calling it *The Dwarfs and Snow White*. As it happened there were nine dwarfs, including a boy who was a dwarf and another who was very tall and lanky. It caused a lot of merriment in the rehearsal and when it was played to an audience.

The writing did not always flow easily; Dorothy had to wait for an inspirational idea at times. At least it was a traditional story, which gave her a framework to mould it around. Once she had written the piece and handed it over to the staff, she took no part in the production. Ann Harris looked after the dramatic side, John Pollard the music and Shirley Wensley worked out the choreography. Other teachers made the costumes and took charge of the artistic work. Many of the children had great singing voices and dramatic ability, so were happy to be involved in the acting, dancing and singing. Some of the teenagers were too self-conscious to take part in that aspect of the production, but they used their talents to the full by painting scenery or helping with the props. One very introverted boy who used a wheelchair, was transformed by being involved in scene painting, for which he had a great flair. It stretched the children, giving them a chance to develop talents they did not know that they possessed. It was also great fun for everyone, and the parents and friends who made up the audience appreciated this fact when they showed their enthusiasm at the end of the show.

Dorothy went on to write four or five more pantomimes for the school. One was *Jack and the Beanstalk*, where she struggled to find a roll for the babies who took part. Eventually she came up with the idea of bean fairies, which was a great success. The Head was always very supportive and became involved in sound effects. He created the right degree of resonance, for the voice of the giant, when Jack encounters him after he climbs the beanstalk. He tried many ways of deepening his voice and eventually recorded the voice of the giant by standing in the empty swimming pool at the school. The booming echo created was just right to suggest a giant.

Another production, and probably the most challenging for Dorothy, was *The Wizard of Oz*. There were the main characters of Dorothy, the Tin Man, the Lion, the Scarecrow, the Wicked Witch of the North and many more, and the small children became the Munchkins. There was no stage in the hall at the school and all the pantomimes had been produced at one end, with the audience at the other. To create the effect of the yellow brick road, the teaching staff involved in the production decided to use the whole hall snaking the road through the audience. As usual it was a triumph and enjoyed by all.

After a few years of being involved in writing these pantomimes the Head, nicknamed Dorothy, the Bard of Sherbourne, as he really appreciated the work she put in voluntarily to help the children enjoy their time at the school. In the early 1980s the National Curriculum began to take up more time, and in July 1986 the school was closed and many of the staff left or retired. Sherbourne Fields reopened in September of that year with a new Head and some new pupils and staff. However, Dorothy did have one more request to write a twenty-minute drama on the theme of *Oliver* a while afterwards. This time it was just one class taking part and despite the constraints of time, all went well. Dorothy received a thank you card from the children in the class, which meant a great deal to her.

That was her last involvement with the school as Lesley had already moved to another school. Dorothy has never forgotten the pleasure of seeing the children in those pantomimes and knowing that it helped the children to widen their interests and display their talents.

Lynn Hockton

Acknowledgements
Thank you to Dorothy Parker and Lesley Grove for sharing their memories of these entertainments.
Dorothy Parker (1913-2008)
Dorothy Parker was a founder member of the Women's Research Group. She was always a great source of information about many aspects of life in Coventry during the twentieth century. We could always draw upon that knowledge when planning one of our books. Sadly Dorothy died in June 2008 at the great age of 95, just as this book was in progress.

Childhood Musings

In life it is often the little things that we remember as well as the big things.

1920s Whip and Top was a popular toy when I was little.

1930s I loved art and wanted to take it up. Each year, at school, when the pupils were   thirteen years old, two were chosen to go to Art School. I was chosen – but I could not go as my mother was ill.

1920s Saturday morning pictures. I used to go to the Cupid (Carlton) Cinema on Stoney Stanton Road.

1930s My mum died when I was fourteen. I was very good at sewing, knitting and art. I wanted to take up art so I went to Art School at night.

1930s I went to see 'Ben Hur' at the pictures, it was in black and white. Suddenly it became coloured. We were all told to leave the cinema in an orderly manner. The Projection Room was on fire and the reflection of the flames on the screen made the film appear to be coloured. All the mums were waiting outside, crying.

1910/20s My brothers were very clever with their hands. They made a radio out of a cocoa tin. When I put the earphones on I could hear Harry Roy and his band playing.

1930s I played the piano when I was young.

1930s We used to go to the allotment for the day and take a picnic - a bottle of water and some bread and butter.

1920s Sometimes I would see a poor old lady pushing a pram, down the street, with a baby in it. People would feel sorry for her and put money into the pram. I was about five at the time and decided that I would try this. I had a toy gramophone and put this into my doll's pram. I had never been allowed out of the garden before, but somehow I got out and off I went down the street. As I went I played a record on the gramophone, one side was: *It Ain't Gonna Rain No More, No More* and the other side was: *The Laughing Policeman*. Well people started to give me money. A little while later I returned home. Mum was very, very cross, all the neighbours had been out looking for me. I got a slap, but she kept the money!

1930s When I was little I inherited my sister's bike. I was given strict instructions not to go out of the street. But I wanted to turn round so I went out on to the Stoney Stanton Road. I got another slap.

Later, when I was twelve, we used to cycle to Leamington and leave our bikes propped up by the gates of Jephson Gardens. They were still there when we came back.

We would also cycle to Stratford and back.

1930s I used to play piano duets with my sister. She played the bass and I played the melody. We both used to sit on the same piano stool until we became too big and we had to find another chair. Father gave me a tin whistle and told me that if I wetted it under the tap it would sound better. One day I came home to find that my mother had stood on it and bent it double. So it went on the back of the fire.

1930/40s I used to stand by the little table in our kitchen and watch my mother cook the Sunday dinner. As I saw her preparing the gravy I knew it would not be long before we ate. When the roast potatoes were cooked she would take them out of the oven and transfer them to the hot cupboard. As she did this she would say to me: 'Get your saucer' and she would give me a roast potato to have before my dinner.

All my life I have loved roast potatoes.

After tea on Sunday, Mum would go next door to have a natter with the neighbour. Then Dad would play with me and my brother. We played lots of games: Blind Man's Buff; One Potato, Two Potato, Three Potato, Four and many more. We had a gramophone with a big green horn and I would put on a headscarf and mime to Gracie Fields' records.

1940s My brothers and I found four wheels from an old pram. We nailed a piece of wood across them to make a seat, and in turn, went careering off down Lythalls Lane, hoping we could stop at the bottom.

1940s Cowboys and Indians was another favourite game and we would have battles with the children in the next garden.

Two pieces of roofing slate made ideal bones (or spoons) to play.

We made our own whip and top.

1940/50s I loved going to the pictures on a Saturday morning. I usually went on my own so on the way back I would try to find a different way each time using as many of the jetties that I could. I don't ever remember walking back along the proper pavements.

1940/50s We played Cowboys and Indians as well, up and down the entries.

The lads would pretend to tie us up.

I used to go scrumping, and we would go blackberrying over the fields at the back. Another game we used to play was: 'What's the time Mr. Wolf?' You were out if you moved and got caught.

1940/50s We put on plays in a neighbour's garage.

One day we were playing hairdressers and the girl next door cut one of the other girl's hair. It was lovely hair and her mother was furious.

1940s I would take my mother's wooden clothes horse into the garden and put it sides down on the ground, like a ridge tent. Throw a blanket over it and weigh it down with bricks either side. That was my house.

There were many bombed buildings and sites when I was a child. I used to spend a lot of time on them playing house with whatever I could find. We also used to build dens using soil.

1940s Take two syrup tins and thread a long piece of string through each. Put one foot on each of the tins, take the strings in your hand and you have a pair of stilts.

1950s We played lots of games in the street. We would sit in the gutter and play Jacks (Snobs, Five Stones) and Hop Scotch on the pavements. Hide and Seek. 'Can We Cross Your Golden River?' Where one person would stand opposite everyone else. We would ask this person 'Can we cross your golden river?' They would reply: 'Yes, if you are wearing red' (or whatever requirement they chose) and so on. There were different games at different times of the year.

1940s In the street we would have a long skipping rope and we would play skipping games. 'All in together', and 'crossing from one side of the rope to the other' while it was being turned.

Or, on your own with a small skipping rope.

1950s At Christmas I would make Christmas decorations with acorns. I would stick pins into an acorn and weave cotton round and round the pins so that it looked like a spider's web.

1950s The Salvation Army would always come round the streets at Christmas and I used to love to listen to them. We always had snow in those days.

1950s We were a large family and at Christmas my aunt from Birmingham would come to visit us. She always brought with her a big Christmas log shaped box and in this box would be lots of little presents each with a number on it. We each chose a number and then picked our present.

1940s On Christmas morning I would always climb into my parents' bed and open my presents with them. One year I kept unwrapping boxes of doll's house furniture and I remember thinking 'What am I going to do with these as I do not have a doll's house?' What a surprise when I went downstairs for there on the table was a beautiful doll's house which my father had made for me. I still have the house and would not part with it.

For a previous Christmas he had made me a Tuck Shop and I had little triangular bags for the sweets and some tiny scales to weigh them on. It was difficult to get toys in the 1940s and I let my Tuck Shop be passed on to another child.

1950s I so wanted a gramophone for Christmas and I hoped against hope that my parents would be able to afford one. The disappointment when I found that my Christmas present was a dressing gown and I remember trying so hard not to let the disappointment show on my face.

1940/50s Throwing a ball up against a wall and catching it. Then two balls, three balls and four if you were clever.

1940s On VE Day we had a street party. There was an apple tree in our garden so our mum made the toffee apples. When she had finished there was a big washing basket full of toffee apples – we were only allowed to have one each!

One day, when mother was out, we tried to make toffee with condensed milk. We burnt a hole in the saucepan!

1950s When I was sixteen I went to the Singer Sewing School in Far Gosford Street to learn how to use a sewing machine. What I gained from this course has stood me in good stead all of my life.

1940/50s It was always my job to shell the peas for Sunday dinner and to make the mint sauce.

1940s A lot of people had allotments in those days and my dad grew rhubarb on his. I would have a piece of newspaper with some sugar in it and dip the rhubarb into the sugar before I ate it.

1950s I loved barley sugar twists.

1940s On the way to school I would buy a pennyworth of Kali from the corner shop. The shopkeeper always put it into a little triangular bag and I would dip my finger into it as I went along.

1940/50s It is smells that remind me of my childhood. Cut grass, creosote, bonfires, real tomatoes – I used to pick the tomatoes in my grandfather's greenhouse.

1940s The radio was part of our lives when we were little. I always listened to Two Way Family Favourites on a Sunday morning.

1940/50s Grandma would play the piano and we would all sit around her and sing.

It always gave me pleasure to sit and look at the family photographs.

1950s I collected pretty stones and swapped them with my friends.

1950s It was so easy to do French Knitting (Corking). A cotton reel with four nails spaced around the top of it and you wove wool in and out of the nails, round and round. One boy, when he had a long string, wound it into a spiral and made a mat.

I loved my mother's button box. I would sort them into colours and sizes.

1950s My father took a group of us from school to the pictures. There was a regular Saturday morning picture show for schools at the Coventry Technical College. On this occasion we saw *Scott of the Antarctic*.

1960/70s One day Mum took my brother and me to the swimming baths. We went with Mum's friend and her children. All of us got changed and headed for the water, except for Mum, who did not like the water and had decided to sit by the side of the pool and watch us. It was my first experience of the swimming baths and down the steps I went – and kept going. Nobody had told me you could not breathe under water! The next minute I was being hauled out by my Mum's friend. Mum was quite oblivious to all of this!

June Hill

Acknowledgements

My heartfelt thanks to: Anne, Dolly, Irene, Jean, Jean, Lesley, Mary, Mary, Pat, Sheila and Suzanne, for their wonderful contributions. When once I posed the question the floodgates of memory were opened wide and the reminiscences came tumbling out.

Volunteering – The Perfect Pastime

In this book, we have looked at various pastimes and entertainments. In both the past and the present, there is one certain way of passing the time – volunteering. There are so many possibilities, so let us consider some of them.

The main object of volunteering is to do something useful or helpful for no payment. There may be someone amongst family, friends and neighbours who need help, either temporarily or long-term, with shopping or walking the dog and many other tasks.

For the athletic, there are many possibilities, such as to run a marathon or a half-marathon: less energetic is a walkathon. Some cycle from Land's End to John O'Groats or various other routes of lesser distance. There is also the very difficult triathlon of swimming, cycling and walking. All these are performed in order to raise money for a good cause and anyone attempting a task of this kind will need to put in a lot of practice and also persuade numerous people to sponsor them, in order to raise enough money to make the whole thing worthwhile.

Have you ever fancied shop work? If so, take a look around the many charity shops in your local shopping area or in the town centre, then call at whichever type of charity appeals to you and you will soon find a vacancy for an assistant for one or more days a week. There will still be time on the other days in the week for your normal activities.

Churches offer endless possibilities for volunteers. Singers can join the choir, which means regular attendance on Sunday, plus choir practice. Similarly, if there is a peal of bells, bell ringers need to be there regularly and attend practice and weddings when required. We must not forget the valiant work of the flower arrangers who make the churches look and smell so beautiful. The church needs cleaning and if it has a churchyard it needs to be kept tidy, hedges require cutting and so on. There will probably be a lunch club for the elderly, so cookery skills are called for, plus helpers to lay the tables, serve the meals and wash up. Tea and coffee need making time and again.

The Boy Scout and Girl Guide movements are totally reliant on volunteers. So if you are capable of keeping boys and girls interested, you might consider offering your services. You will need to spend quite a lot of time thinking what you are going to do, in addition to the actual meetings. Here is also the possibility of taking part in a camping expedition.

You could consider volunteering at Walsgrave Hospital. Volunteers man the kiosk at the Arden Cancer Centre; profits being used to buy extra items for the comfort of patients. They also run the hospital radio, greet people at reception and help them find their way around. This will occupy either a whole day or a half-day per week.

There are numerous tasks that do not require such regular attention, a litter-picker for example. This can do wonders for a local open space and if you can get whole families involved, it helps the children to take pride in keeping their whole area clean and tidy.

Towards Christmas all sorts of organisations hold bazaars. They will be glad of help and not only on the day. So if you are good at making cakes and jam, pickling onions, thinking up competitions or enjoy selling, they would be glad of your help.

No one need ever feel bored and unoccupied, for there is always a way of filling time as a volunteer and in the process of helping others, gain satisfaction for yourself.

Lynn has been a reader to the blind for over ten years now. She was assigned to a young woman working full-time and went to her place of work once a week, to read her personal correspondence and help with some work-related tasks. This continued for nearly six years until her listener left work to have a baby daughter. Since then Lynn has read to her or her husband, who is also blind, in their own home. It requires a commitment to become a reader, but it is not an onerous task, in fact you become a friend of the family. This couple and their daughter are a delight to be with, they have a great sense of humour and reading to them can be a lot of fun. As Lynn says, it has enriched her life in a way that she never imagined when she first volunteered.

Angela has been a volunteer for many years in several different organisations. Her first involvement came through membership of Moose International, where at one point she became Lady Chairman of the Ladies Circle. They organised whist drives, craft fairs, jumble sales and many more events to raise money for charity. They took children from deprived areas of the city on day trips, organised parties for disabled children and an annual dinner for housebound people with transport to the Lodge room.

When Angela's father died in 1981, she took a donation to Coventry Stroke Group, as her father had suffered a severe stroke thirteen years before. She was asked if she would like to help out with the group and she agreed despite the work she was already doing for Moose. Little did she know that she would spend the next twenty-seven years as a volunteer for Coventry Stroke Group, almost immediately becoming Treasurer and then as Chairman for over twenty years. It finally closed in 2008 due to lack of support from Social Services. Angela has always been generous with her time despite working full-time for most of those years, before retirement. (See our book *Telling Tales* for a fuller account of Angela's work with Moose and Coventry Stroke Group).

After many years as a secondary school teacher, Ann retired at the age of 59. She was really looking forward to lazy days doing very little, but after three months she was desperate to occupy her time again. She had always been a supporter of Oxfam and the work they did for disadvantaged people in the third world. Oxfam were always first on the scene in an emergency or disaster, usually setting up water supplies for local people. So when she saw an advertisement in the local paper for volunteers, she decided to apply. She was particularly interested in one of the jobs – recruiting volunteers to work in shops. This meant travelling to various shops in the Midlands, however, travelling expenses were reimbursed.

The areas for which Ann was responsible were Oxfordshire and Hereford and Worcester and she worked for two days a week. It was an early start to travel to some of the shops and then setting up in a space where there was enough room to display leaflets and flyers. Then the hard work began. Shoppers were approached and chatted to, eventually working round to the fact that the shop needed volunteers. Most people were ready to listen and many were willing to help, either dealing with customers on the counter or sorting clothes, books and bric-a-brac. Some volunteers became expert in particular fields, such as jewellery and books, and some were very possessive of their 'department.'

One way of recruiting, which Ann found particularly successful, was to organise a special event such as a 'birthday celebration.' She would write to the local Mayor and ask if he or she could attend, giving the time and date. Most Mayors were only too willing to accept, as the local papers and radio stations were invited, so it was good publicity for them as well as the shop. Ann always made a cake and tea and coffee were offered. The event attracted a lot of attention and people having a cup of tea and a cake are more willing to sign up as a volunteer!

There was contact with other recruiters from time to time where discussion took place as to the best ways of recruiting and what had worked and what had not. Some volunteers were good at designing posters and these could be produced on coloured paper for display in the shop, to remind shoppers that

Tea and cake at an Oxfam event.

volunteers were always needed. When Ann was targeting a particular Oxfam shop, she would spend some time in the town displaying posters and quite often it was possible to do a display in the local library, with photographs of some of the projects Oxfam was involved in.

Volunteering is a very satisfying job. Working in a shop makes you get out of the house and gives you a chance to meet lots of people – both work colleagues and regular customers. It is also a stepping-stone for those people who are searching for paid work. If you can prove that you have been using your spare time to help others, then an employer will often take this into consideration. However, you must be very strict with yourself and resist buying the stock. Ann regularly returned home from her visits with 'bargains'.

The Women's Research Group comprises of members who work voluntarily to produce books about women of Coventry in the twentieth century. It takes time and effort to interview women about their lives and work, research those who are no longer alive or investigate a topic of interest for inclusion in our books. Interviews and information gathered are then written up in a readable form that is intended to be enjoyable and informative. It would not exist without volunteers and all those stories would be lost.

Kathleen Barker, Lynn Hockton and Ann Waugh